THE INCARNATION
──────── of ────────
TRUTH

THE INCARNATION
of
TRUTH

The Word Became Flesh
and Dwelt Among Us

FREDERICK GORINI

TATE PUBLISHING
AND ENTERPRISES, LLC

Published by Tate Publishing & Enterprises, LLC
127 E. Trade Center Terrace | Mustang, Oklahoma 73064 USA
1.888.361.9473 | www.tatepublishing.com

Tate Publishing is committed to excellence in the publishing industry. The company reflects the philosophy established by the founders, based on Psalm 68:11,
"The Lord gave the word and great was the company of those who published it."

Book design copyright © 2014 by Tate Publishing, LLC. All rights reserved.
Cover design by Errol Villamante
Interior design by Caypeeline Casas

Published in the United States of America

ISBN: 978-1-62902-518-6
1. Religion / General
2. Religion / Christian Life / General
13.11.27

OTHER BOOKS BY THE AUTHOR:

To the Unknown God
The One whom you worship without
knowing, Him I proclaim to you.

Truth Be Told

Truth about Lies

DEDICATION

To whoever will believe.
It was inspired by Dr. Jay Leroux.

CONTENTS

PREFACE

It is high time for Christians to get back to the Bible. We have allowed our culture to reduce the message of God's word. I ask you to take a journey with me into a threefold revelation of truth. Before we take the first step, I would like to administer a simple test.

The Question: Why did the Word of God become flesh and dwell among us?
The Answer: To take away our sins (*most* Christians would know this).
The Grade: Incomplete (as opposed to incorrect).

I repeat:
The Question: Why did the Word of God become flesh and dwell among us?
The Answer: To destroy the works of the devil (*some* Christians might know this).
The Grade: Incomplete (as opposed to incorrect).

Once more I ask:
The Question: Why did the Word of God become flesh and dwell among us?
The Answer: Let's find out!
The Grade: To be determined (by you!).

Please note that I have filled these pages not only with my own words but with numerous references to the word of God. At best, my words can only help you to discover what God's Word really says. Please read God's Word.

I have also written certain things more than once, sometimes over and over and over again. Repetition is a valuable part of learning. It is part of the process of meditation that leads to a renewed mind and the subsequent transformation into the image of Christ.

Join me on this journey to mature in Christ. It has the potential to change your life to such a degree that you can become a vital part of the company of redeemed men, women, and children who are literally changing the world. After all, *God* is our Father.

Walk with me, as I am learning to walk with him.

> May the LORD bless you and keep you; the LORD make His face shine upon you, and be gracious to you; the LORD lift up His countenance upon you, and give you peace.
>
> Numbers 6:24–26

PROLOGUE

So that your trust may be in the LORD; I have instructed you today, even you. Have I not written to you excellent things of counsels and knowledge, that I may make you know the certainty of the words of truth, that you may answer words of truth to those who send you?

Proverbs 22:19-21

A threefold cord is not quickly broken.

Ecclesiastes 4:12b

I think it proper to begin this journey into truth with a brief introduction to a scriptural and spiritual principle. This principle concerns the threefold revelation of truth found in the Scriptures and throughout all of creation.

The writer of Proverbs 22 said that he wrote "excellent things" to the reader. He did this so that the reader might be certain of the truth. In times like these, certainty is an essential part of survival and effective ministry. We must have truthful answers to the questions that we as believers are asking and being asked by those searching for a reality in God. Only the knowledge of the truth can make men free.[1]

The word translated as "excellent" in the Proverb quoted above is actually the Hebrew word "shaliysh." This Hebrew word defines something that is triangular or threefold. It is derived from the Hebrew word for the number three.[2] This is a very important concept that will help us to understand the certainty of truth.

The Bible is full of references to truth that appear in a threefold form. God himself is revealed to us as Father, Son, and Holy Spirit.[3] He is referred to as life, light, and love.[4] Since God created man in his own image and likeness,[5] man is also a triune being, being comprised of spirit, soul, and body.[6] Desirous to have an intimate relationship with man, God established a mandatory, and minimum, threefold appointment schedule between man and himself.

In Old Testament Scripture, God commanded all men of faith to meet with him annually on three occasions: the Feast of Unleavened Bread, the Feast of Weeks, and the Feast of Tabernacles.[7] The meeting place was also patterned after a triune revelation. There was an outer court, an inner court, and a court called the Holiest of All.[8] In this meeting place, there were three kinds of light: natural light in the outer court, the light of the lampstand in the inner court, and the light of God's own presence above the mercy seat in the Holiest place of all.[9]

The New Testament understanding and application of this threefold place of meeting between God and man could be considered to be the body (the outer court), the soul (the inner court), and the spirit (the Holiest of All) of man. Since Jesus taught his disciples to pray (meet with) and ask the Father for "daily" bread,[10] we could apply our New Testament understanding to the Old Testament annual appointments to meet with God as being morning, noon, and night on a "daily" basis. Think about it, in almost every culture of the world, these three times of the day are usually the times set aside for partaking of a meal.

This triune or threefold pattern of "excellence" is used throughout the Word of God to reveal truth. Consider that our Lord Jesus Christ is anointed as prophet, priest, and king.[11] He is called the way, the truth, and the life.[12] Jesus is also called the Word of God[13] and the ministry of the Word is likened to feeding with bread, milk, and meat.[14]

Spiritual growth in the kingdom of God is also revealed in a threefold manner. Using an agricultural analogy, Jesus said that first comes the blade, then the head, and after that the full grain in the head.[15] He taught that kingdom fruit is also brought forth in a threefold measure—some thirtyfold, some sixty, and some a hundred.[16] It has always been God's will for man to be fruitful.[17]

The covenant blessing of fruitfulness promised to the Old Testament patriarch Abraham is also revealed in a threefold manner. The seed of Abraham is described as being as numerous as the dust of the earth, the sand of the sea, and the stars of heaven.[18] In the New Testament, the apostle Paul also used a threefold analogy to describe the will of God. He declared God's will to be good, acceptable, and perfect.[19]

It is amazing just how often this presentation of truth in an excellent, threefold way is found in the Scriptures. Even the kingdom economy of God has a threefold measure of covenant giving woven within it.

Believers present tithes and offerings to the Lord and alms to the poor to honor the Lord.[20]

God's witness to man concerning all that he has created is also presented in an excellent, threefold way. Our entire world view is based upon the knowledge, understanding, and wisdom provided by the author of our faith, Jesus Christ. The apostle John revealed that this witness or testimony of God to man, both in heaven and on earth, share a threefold agreement as one. He said,

> There are three who bear witness in heaven: the Father, the Word, and the Holy Spirit; and these three are one. And there are three that bear witness on earth: the Spirit, the water, and the blood; and these three agree as one.[21]

Each of these expressions of truth is revealed as a threefold cord intimately woven together as one. Remember that God reveals truth in this way so that we may be certain of it, without doubting.[22] The writer of the book of Ecclesiastes wrote that two are better than one[23] and a threefold cord is not easily undone.[24]

There are so many more examples of the threefold revelation of truth that can be found in the Scriptures. I encourage you to search them out. It is an exciting journey. The final example that I would like to point out to you is from the book of Job.

In Chapter 33, Job's friend Elihu is engaged in a very important discourse with Job concerning his self justification. Job's other three friends, Zophar, Eliphaz, and Bildad, had found no answer concerning Job's trials.[25] We could say that their three opinions did not come together as a threefold revelation of truth concerning Job.

Elihu admonished and encouraged Job that God was surely at work in his circumstances. He declared that God was indeed in control, establishing truth in Job's life that would keep back his soul from the Pit and his life from perishing by the sword.[26] Elihu declared that the words he was speaking to Job were pure knowledge from an upright heart that were inspired by God.[27] He declared,

> For God may speak in one way, or in another, yet man does not perceive it. In a dream, in a vision of the night, when deep sleep falls upon men, while slumbering on their beds, then He opens the ears of men, and seals their instruction.[28]

It is obvious that God wants man to know the truth and be saved and set free by it. The account is so rich and full of wisdom. The summation of Elihu's discourse is this:

> Behold, God works all these things, twice, in fact, three times with a man, to bring back his soul from the Pit, that he may be enlightened with the light of life.[29]

There can be no question about it. The Lord God communicates truth to every man twice—in fact, three times! He wants us to be certain of the truth and have it established in the foundation of our faith. It is the knowledge of the excellence of truth that sets us free and saves us from the Pit.

Look around. Smell the roses, as some would say. Even our natural world is patterned after a threefold revelation. We describe the world we live in as being made up of time, space, and matter. Time itself is experienced as past, present, and future, isn't that right? Space is measured in length, width, and depth. Everything visible to the natural eye is measured in three dimensions. We describe matter as being either solid, liquid, or gas. We all experience something as basic as H_2O in the forms of ice, water, and steam. There is something awesome at work here! Because of the nature of these things, we can be sure that a threefold revelation of truth brings certainty.

Now take a giant step with me. I ask you, "Why then did the Eternal Word become the Incarnate Word and invade the world of men? What is the threefold revelation of the purpose of the manifestation of Christ in this world? What is the message hidden in the threefold incarnation of truth?"

It is written, "Ask, and it will be given to you; seek, and you will find; knock, and it will be opened to you."[30] Whatever your stage of growth in maturing in Christ, you can be sure that Creator God, our loving Father, has left you a message that will become the incarnation of truth in your own life as you read on. Just do it!

> I write unto you little children. I write unto you young men. I write unto you Fathers.
>
> 1 John 2:12–14 (Paraphrased excerpts)

PROLOGUE

MAIN POINTS:

- Biblical truth is revealed in an excellent, three-fold way.
- This provides certainty for the believer.
- God wants man to know the truth.
- It is the knowledge of truth that saves men and sets them free.
- The incarnation of the Eternal Word of God can be understood in a threefold revelation.

THE QUESTIONS

In the beginning was the Word, and the Word
was with God, and the Word was God. And the
Word became flesh and dwelt among us, and
we beheld His glory, the glory as of the only
begotten of the Father, full of grace and truth.

John 1:1, 14

Call to Me, and I will answer you, and show
you great and mighty things, which you do not
know.

Jeremiah 33:3

Who among us has not asked, "Why?" The answer to
this significant question gives a meaning and purpose
to everything. It is one of the six one-word questions
of all time. Who? What? When? Where? How? Why?
Throughout the ages, all of mankind has asked these
universal questions. I'm sure you have asked them
also. Asking such questions seems to be a part of our
human DNA.

Is it possible for anyone to really answer such questions truthfully without knowing the Person of truth?
According to the Holy Scriptures, Jesus Christ is truth
personified.[1]

In the Word of God, Jesus is called the Alpha and
Omega, the Beginning and the End, the author and
finisher of our faith.[2] Hence, we need to look to him
as the Incarnate Word and the author of the Holy

Scriptures to find meaningful answers to these questions. The Bible, which is written to testify of Christ,[3] is the only authorized source for answers to these, and all of life's mysteries and questions.

The Word of God provides a manifold revelation of truth for us. The Bible could be considered a prescription for our well-being. The apostle Paul wrote to the church at Rome saying, "For whatever things were written before were written for our learning, that we through the patience and comfort of the Scriptures might have hope."[4]

That which was written before could be considered to be a "pre" (before) "scription" (to write) provided by God for us.

There are many Scriptures that one could find to answer these very important questions. A brief look at the first chapter of Ephesians will give us a starting place. Other starting places and references are also hidden in God's Word. I encourage you to search for them. You will be amazed at what you find.

Let's begin by taking these questions one at a time and finding the revelation that Paul shared with the church at Ephesus. Remember, at first our answers will be very brief. Then we will launch into the deep to find a fuller revelation of the biblical answers to these questions.

In his epistle to the saints in Ephesus, Paul addressed the question, "Who?" He wrote, "The God and Father of our Lord Jesus Christ."[5] God the Father is the ultimate "who." Our Lord Jesus Christ, as his only begotten Son, being One with the Father is also part of the answer to "who?"[6] It would also be advantageous at this point to remember and acknowledge the Holy Spirit who is also an integral part of the Godhead.[7]

"Who" did "what"? "What" has God done and what does he continue to do? Paul wrote that God "has blessed us with every spiritual blessing in the heavenly places in Christ."[8] Not only does this revelation provide an answer to "what?" but it also includes "us" in the answer to the question "who?" As you continue to read, you will discover that the angelic creatures of the heavenly realm also play an important role of understanding the answers to our questions.[9] Let's continue to ask more questions.

"When" did God bless us and choose us? The answer will astound you. Paul wrote, "… before the foundation of the world."[10] This is truly amazing. However, the Scripture clearly describes God's ability to do something as unusual as completing something "before" it has begun. It is a demonstration of his omniscience and omnipotence. God declared about himself,

> I am God, and there is no other; I am God, and
> there is no one like Me, declaring the end from
> the beginning, and from ancient times things
> that are not yet done, saying, 'My counsel shall
> stand, and I will do all my pleasure.'[11]

God does indeed have an eternal purpose that he has declared and set into motion from the beginning.[12] As I have noted, he is called the Alpha and Omega, the beginning and the end.[13]

"Where" does all this take place? The answer to this question must include the revelation of the relationship between the heavens and the earth. In the beginning, God created the heavens and the earth.[14] This is the first statement made in the Holy Scriptures. Through his teachings concerning prayer to God the Father, Jesus revealed that it is God's will and intention for the earth to be a mirror image of heaven. He said, "In this manner, therefore, pray: Our Father in heaven, Hallowed be Your name. Your kingdom come. Your will be done on earth as it is in heaven."[15]

God works from his throne in heaven.[16] This is his original dwelling place.[17] Paul identified the source from which every spiritual blessing of God given to man comes from. Revealing the answer to the question of "where," Paul wrote, "…in the heavenly places in Christ."[18]

God's blessings to man originate in the heavens but are manifested on earth, in man, in and through Christ. By Christ, all things were created that are in heaven and on earth. All things were created through him and for him.[19] Whatever takes place in the heavens directly affects what takes place on the earth. The heaven of heavens is where God's throne is. The earth is his footstool, the place of his rest, where his will, his work, and his blessings are directed.[20] Really? Yes, really!

"How" does all this come together and actually work? The "how" of things speaks of understanding, not just knowledge. We can express our understanding of how God works by identifying four significant historical acts:

- The Creation (of all things)[21]
- The Fall (of man)[22]
- The Redemption (through Christ)[23]
- The Restoration (of all things)[24]

The redemption of all things that have been affected by transgression against God is the means through which God fulfills the blessing of man. Concerning just "how" God does this, Paul wrote, by adopting us to himself through Jesus Christ and redeeming us to himself by Christ's blood.[25] There is no other way for redemption to take place. Jesus himself said, "I am the way, the truth, and the life."[26] No one can come to the Father except through the redemptive blood of Jesus Christ.[27] This is a hard saying for some to accept; nevertheless, it stands true as God's answer to "how?"

Someone might ask, "What if someone in a remote part of our planet never hears the good news of Jesus Christ, the incarnation of truth? How can they be saved and come to the Father?" These are very good and important questions. Please read the Epistle of Paul to the Romans, Chapter 2 vv. 11–16 for clarity. I will leave it to you to search the matter out. Let's continue and find out "why?"

"Why" does God want to adopt us, redeem us, bless us? Paul made it very clear when he wrote, "...that we should be holy and without blame before him in love."[28] God is Holy.[29] His purpose and plan always intended for all of his children to also be holy as he is.[30] Man was created in the image and likeness of a Holy God.[31] Think of "holy" as being pure, the way we were in the beginning before the fall.

These words of Paul, through scriptural insights from God's authorized source of truth, provide answers to these six intriguing questions. Of course, each answer begs a fuller revelation. Remember the answers to these questions have only been expressed in brevity. They are taken from a few verses in Paul's epistle to the Ephesian believers. It is the glory of God to conceal answers and the glory of royalty to search for the answers.[32] Before we can find satisfactory answers, we must sincerely ask the right questions. Asking such questions is the beginning of our training in becoming part of God's royal family!

"Why?" certainly is an essential question. The answers to Who? What? Where? When? and How? do not completely satisfy until one knows why. "Why" speaks to purpose—to reason. Without purpose or reason everything else is somewhat irrelevant.

Twenty years ago, an anointed teacher of God's Word taught us that finding and fulfilling our purpose in life is the only way to preserve and be blessed by God's original intention for creating us. He taught us that God is a God of purpose. Everything in life has a purpose. When purpose is not known, abuse (abnormal use) is inevitable. To find the purpose of something, you must ask its creator. Purpose can only be found in the mind of the creator. It is finding true purpose that preserves the purity and sanctity of one's life.[33]

Not only does finding purpose preserve one's life, it significantly enhances it. If you don't know why you are you, how can you hope to reach your full potential, and as the United States Army says, "Be all that you can be"? How much higher is God's plan for you than any plan that an army of man can contrive?

My goal is not to teach about natural things but spiritual ones. I want to emphasize the purpose in the mind of the Creator God, the Father of our Lord Jesus Christ, when he made all that is—and when he made us. As I recount what I have discovered concerning the secrets of God's covenant with man,[34] you may become aware of a much greater purpose for your own life than ever before.

"The secret things belong to the LORD, but those things which are revealed belong to us and to our children...."[35] God reveals his plans for us to us so that we may fulfill the purpose for which he created us. As you read, pray for the spirit of wisdom and revelation in the knowledge of God, as Paul did for the church at Ephesus.[36] God wants us to know the hope of his calling, what the riches of the glory of his inheritance is in us, and the exceeding greatness of his power toward us who believe.[37]

The apostle Paul received revelation of these mysteries to make them known to all people.[38] God does not only want all people to share the revelation of the fellowship of the mystery of Christ—he wants his manifold wisdom to be made known by the church (those in the fellowship) to the principalities and powers in the heavenly places.[39]

This is to be done according to the eternal purpose which God accomplished in our Lord Jesus Christ.[40] "It is finished!" Christ declared from the cross.[41] "It is done!" declared he who sits on the throne forever.[42] The outcome is not in question. The foundation of the eternal purpose of God stands sure.[43] The Lord declares that we are his chosen witnesses—that we may know and believe him.[44]

The Lord has sent us his Holy Spirit, the guarantee of our inheritance[45] and of our eternal habitation[46] that we may know him and also make him known. We have received power to be his witnesses in all the earth.[47]

It is high time for God's people to awake out of sleep, for our salvation is nearer than when we first believed.[48] It is time to know the answers to Who? What? When? Where? How? Why? Only then can we make the mystery of Christ known to all men and the manifold wisdom of God known to the principalities and powers in the heavenly places.[49]

All of these six questions are intricately woven together. The "how?" is especially connected to the "why?" God's ultimate intention for man is that we should be holy and without blame before him in love.[50] How does he accomplish such a destiny in man, especially after the fall in the garden of Eden?

The answer as we have seen is that God adopts us as his children by first redeeming us to himself through the blood of Christ.[51] We could say that the "how" and "why" could be summed up in one short statement— the incarnation of truth.

Why was the Eternal Word made to be the Incarnate Word? How does the incarnation answer the questions: Why did God create me? What is my purpose? What is my purpose in light of God's eternal purpose? How should I live now?

The Lord God has written the answers. Read on, dear one, and read the Scripture references as you do. In them you will find the testimony of the Lord Jesus Christ (the Incarnate Word). You will find that his words are spirit and life.[52] You will find truth. The truth will set you free.[53] Free to be who God always intended for you to be. Thank God that he has written such a wonderful prescription for us![54]

> I write to you, little children, because your sins are forgiven you for His name's sake. I write to you, fathers, because you have known Him who is from the beginning. I write to you, young men, because you have overcome the wicked one. I write to you, little children, because you have known the Father. I have written to you, fathers, because you have known Him who is from the beginning. I have written to you, young men, because you are strong, and the word of God abides in you, and you have overcome the wicked one.
>
> 1 John 2:12–14

THE QUESTIONS
MAIN POINTS:

- There are six one word questions common to man: Who? What? When? Where? How? Why?
- God's word is a "pre-scription" for us.
- The first chapter of Ephesians is a good starting place to find answers to these questions.
- Four significant, historical events are: The Creation, The Fall, The Redemption, and The Restoration.
- Finding purpose preserves and enhances life.
- The eternal purpose of God accomplished in Christ is to make the mystery of Christ known to all people and through the church make his manifold wisdom known to the inhabitants of the spiritual heavenly realm.
- The "how" and "why" of the redemption of man can be summed up in one short statement—the incarnation of truth.

THE LITTLE CHILDREN

The life was manifested, and we have seen and
bear witness, and declare to you that eternal life
which was with the Father and was manifested
to us.

1 John 1:2

But as many as received Him, to them he gave
the right to become children of God, to those
who believe in His name.

John 1:12

The Word became flesh and dwelt among us.[1] Why?
What was the purpose for the Word of God to come
out of eternity and be made manifest in the world of
time and space? Almost all Christians would give the
same answer. It is a good answer. It is true, but it is
incomplete when presented by itself.

Believers would quote the Scripture and declare,
"And you know that He was manifested to take away
our sins, and in Him there is no sin."[2] Thank God for
what we know! However, it is often what we don't know
that can harm us. Keep this in mind as you read on.

Because we have the written word of God, we
know that we were not redeemed to God with cor-
ruptible things like silver or gold.[3] We know that we
were redeemed with and by the precious blood of Jesus
Christ, the Lamb of God without blemish or spot.[4]

It is written,

> But He was wounded for our transgressions,
> He was bruised for our iniquities; the chastise-
> ment for our peace was upon Him, and by His
> stripes we are healed. All we like sheep have
> gone astray; we have turned, every one, to his
> own way; and the LORD has laid on Him the
> iniquity of us all.[5]

Thank God that we have not neglected such a great salvation![6]

According to the word of God, all men "have sinned and fall short of the glory of God."[7] The sin nature was inherited from the first man, Adam.[8] The Eternal Word had to become the Incarnate Word to save us from the condemnation of the law of sin and death in the eyes of a Holy God.[9]

This is true and wonderful, but keep in mind the result of sin was that man fell short of the eternal purpose for his being—the glory of God![10] Meditate for a moment on this statement. It will resurface in a magnificent revelation of truth as the picture of God's eternal purpose is developed in the light of God's Word.

The fall of man did not take God by surprise. As Creator of all things, God indeed knew that the first man, Adam, would sin. He made provision for man's redemption long before the fall ever happened. Before the foundation of the world, God the Father foreordained that Jesus Christ, his Son, would be manifest as the Incarnate Word in these last times "to give His life a ransom for many."[11]

There was to be only one mediator between God and men, the man Jesus Christ, who gave himself for the salvation of all—for whoever would believe in him.[12] This is why the prophet John the Baptist cried out, "Behold the Lamb of God who takes away the sin of the world!"[13]

Yes, Jesus, the Christ, the Eternal Word, was manifested to take away our sins.[14] In the predetermined counsel of God, before the foundation of the world, we who believe were chosen to be holy and blameless (without sin) before him in love.[15]

Indeed, this is how the love of God was manifested towards us. God sent his only begotten son into the world to be the propitiation for our sins.[16] According to the foreknowledge of God the Father, we were chosen to be cleansed from our sins by the blood of Jesus.[17]

There can be no doubt about it. Why was the Eternal Word of God manifest in time and space? It was to take away our sins.[18] This was the great plan of salvation through which God restored eternal life to all who believe in Jesus Christ.[19]

This eternal life was promised to us before time began.[20] According to the eternal plan of God, this hope of eternal life and the manifestation of his Word in time and space occurs through preaching.[21] It is the proclamation of God's eternal truth in our time and space world. This is in complete accord with the creation principles of the book of Genesis. Concerning the creation of all that is, it is written, "Then God said… And God saw…."[22] God saw nothing until God said.

For this reason, the apostle Paul said, "For I am not ashamed of the gospel [good news] of Christ, for it is the power of God to salvation for everyone who believes."[23]

God has chosen the foolishness of preaching (proclaiming the truth) to save those who believe.[24]

It is essential that we tell everyone why the Eternal, Incarnate Word of God was manifest in time and space. The power of the gospel is included and activated in it's proclamation![25] Without announcing it, no one can experience it. We must never be ashamed of our testimony and witness of the good news.[26] God has "saved us and called us with a holy calling, not according to our works, but according to His own purpose and grace which was given to us in Christ Jesus before time began."[27]

This truth has been clearly revealed by the appearing (the manifestation) of our Savior Jesus Christ in our time and space world.[28] Through his incarnation, death, burial, resurrection, and ascension, he has saved us from our sins, abolished death, and brought life and immortality to light through the gospel.[29]

There can be no doubt; no confusion about it. The Holy Scriptures are clear in stating that Jesus Christ has come out of eternity, appearing in our time and space world, to put away sin by the sacrifice of himself.[30] We must be established in this gospel truth and preach Jesus Christ to all men according to the revelation of the mystery which was once kept secret but now has been made manifest by the prophetic scriptures.[31]

However, we must preach not only this beginning of truth but the whole counsel of God. This wonderful truth that Jesus Christ was manifested to save us from our sins is not the entire answer to why the Eternal Word came and dwelt among us.[32] We must continue (abide) in God's Word if we are to know the truth and be set free by it.[33]

In his farewell to the church elders at Miletus, the apostle Paul said, "I kept back nothing [from you] that was helpful, but proclaimed it to you and taught you—the whole counsel of God."[34] A modern day saying goes something like this, "Halfway is no way at all."[35] We have also heard something like, "Half full is the same as half empty."[36] It is time for the church to receive the revelation of the whole counsel of God not just a part of it.

Becoming the children of God whose sins are forgiven by receiving Christ[37] is only the first part of the answer to "Why?" Almost all Christians can tell you this part of the answer to such a profound and important question. However, only a few have come to a fuller revelation of the reason for the incarnation.

This failure to continue in God's Word has stunted the growth of the church and weakened our witness of Christ in the world. It makes our gospel appear to be limited to an after-death reconciliation with the Creator God. It has caused our preaching to be somewhat like offering fire insurance to people for a time in the distant future when this life is over.

This partial answer to the purpose that Christ was manifested in this world does not help us live a life here in time and space that attracts unbelievers to God. We appear too powerless in this life, having only a hope for a better life in the "sweet by and by." This is a tragedy.

This level of Christian living has been negatively influenced by the wiles of the devil.[38] We should not be ignorant of his devices.[39] If he cannot get us to reject the word of God, his next order of temptation is to get us to reduce it. Let me give you a vivid illustration.

Many years ago, while baptizing a newly born-again believer, the reduction of our Christian faith became clearer to me than ever before. I asked the person being baptized if there was anything she would like to say. She responded with a testimony to this effect:

> Having been brought up in the Christian faith, in a Christian home, I always knew that in the end, when I died, Jesus would be there for me. Now, having been born again, I have received a fuller revelation of Christ; I know that he is here for me every day![40]

Wow, what a difference such a revelation can make in someone's life!

It is high time for us to come out of the future and into the present with our faith! We must learn to trust the Lord not only after this life is over, but also trust him every day—in every way. Not only is there life after death—there is life after birth! Having received Christ, we have indeed been "born again"![41] Let's live—now!

Jesus Christ was manifested to take away our sins and make each of us a new creation in him.[42] Eternal life begins right now for those that receive the Lord

Jesus and become children of God. This new life in Christ offers us amazing opportunities to glorify God.

Our Heavenly Father is glorified as we outgrow and put away childish things and mature enough to bear the fruit of his kingdom on earth.[43] Would it not be tragic to celebrate the life of a newborn child only to realize that the child was born with a birth defect that would cause it to remain in a state of infancy all its life? Such a child would never be able to mature to the place of adulthood and become a viable and vital part of a family and a society. Certainly you would agree that this would be a tragedy.

Such is the case with so many members of the Body of Christ that have been born again. Coming to and growing no further than the revelation that Christ was manifest in the flesh to take away our sins has caused a serious and crippling level of immaturity among the children of God. Remaining in an infantile state after being born again short circuits the believer's ability to mature and bear fruit unto God. It can actually bring doubt as to whether such a one has really been born again.

Bearing fruit unto God brings him glory.[44] Read it! Without bearing fruit unto God, the born-again believer, though redeemed by the blood of Christ, remains in the condition of falling short of the glory of God in the same way that an unbeliever does. As it is written, "All have sinned and fall short of the glory of God."[45] How many who attend our churches are in this condition?

Though forgiven of sins, there is no real change in the lifestyle of an immature believer. There is little or no spiritual growth to distinguish a believer from a non-believer. This condition was described by Jesus in what is known as the parable of the sower—the greatest of all parables.[46]

Jesus described this condition with words such as one who received seed "among thorns…that choke the word."[47] Thorns are indicative of the curse put on the earth by God as the consequence of man's rebellion and fall from grace.[48]

In the Old Testament, God warned his people that if they did not take the next step (a step of maturity) after entering the Promised Land and drive out its inhabitants, the consequences would be tragic. The Lord declared that their failure to drive out the sinful inhabitants of the land (those who were falling short of the glory of God) would lead to those same inhabitants becoming irritants to the eyes of the people and thorns in their sides.[49] He even said it would cause him to do to them, His own people, what he originally intended to do to the sinners![50] Read it! Please…

This tragedy was to take place in the newly entered Promised Land. Even though God's people had been delivered from bondage in Egypt and the many years of wilderness wandering, they would still suffer the consequences of failing to mature beyond infancy.

It is no different for those in the New Covenant. After being born again as children of God, if there is no growth to maturity, the children, though forgiven of sins, are still subject to the devices of evil. This is not the will of God but the work of the devil. Because of this, the blessings provided by God are deferred and held in reserve until a later time. The release of the blessings awaits the maturing of the believer. A child of God overcomes the wicked one by advancing beyond infancy into adulthood.

The words written by the apostle John make this truth very clear. He wrote,

> I write to you, little children, because your sins are forgiven you for His name's sake. I write to you, young men, because you have overcome the wicked one.[51]

Carefully notice the difference between little children and young men. Young men (adults) are overcomers in this life. Obviously, God intends for his children to grow beyond the state of infancy. In the book of Revelation, seven wonderful blessings are pronounced for those who mature and overcome. The Lord makes these promises to them:

- To him who overcomes, I will give to eat from the tree of life, which is in the midst of the Paradise of God.[52]
- He who overcomes shall not be hurt by the second death.[53]
- To him who overcomes, I will give some of the hidden manna to eat. And I will give him a white stone, and on the stone a new name written which no one knows except him who receives it.[54]

- And he who overcomes, and keeps my works until the end, to him I will give power over the nations—…and I will give him the morning star.[55]
- He who overcomes shall be clothed in white garments, and I will not blot out his name from the Book of Life; but I will confess his name before my Father and before his angels.[56]
- He who overcomes, I will make him a pillar in the temple of my God, and he shall go out no more. I will write on him the name of my God and the name of the city of my God, the New Jerusalem, which comes down out of heaven from my God. And I will write on him my new name.[57]
- To him who overcomes, I will grant to sit with me on my throne, as I also overcame and sat down with my Father on his throne.[58]

These promises are awesome but will not be experienced in a significant measure in this life for those who remain infants. I recognize that the fullness of these blessings may not be experienced in totality until a certain "fullness of time." However, those who mature certainly can expect, in this life, to taste "the good word of God and the powers of the age to come."[59]

Those who remain as infants, simply "little children" in this life, can only be fed with milk and not solid food. They are found to be unskilled in the word of righteousness—merely "babes."[60] Their childish (not childlike) lifestyle, which is not much different than the world's, brings no fruit to maturity to the glory of God.

Once again, the words of Jesus in the great parable make it very clear: "The ones that fell among thorns… bring no fruit to maturity."[61] To describe such an immature lifestyle, Jesus used the following phrases to explain the spiritual meaning of the thorns that choke the word:

- The cares of this world[62]
- The deceitfulness of riches[63]
- The desires for other things[64]
- The pleasures of this life[65]

Although these phrases are self explanatory, it would be good to pause here and evaluate your own ability and track record in overcoming such "thorns." How important are such things to you? How tight is their grip upon your fruit-bearing potential?

It is very simple. No fruit—no glory! The sinner falls short of the glory of God. The infantile believer brings no fruit to maturity and thereby also falls short of the glory of God. God is glorified when the believer bears much fruit. It is very simple.

It was always God's intention to bring many sons to glory as it is written:

> For it was fitting for Him [God], for whom are all things and by whom are all things, in bringing many sons to glory, to make the captain of their salvation [Jesus] perfect through sufferings [the sufferings of the tasting of death required by the sin of man].[66]

Remember, the Scripture declares that we know that our sins were taken away for his name's sake.[67] Salvation doesn't do something for us alone; God himself is glorified as we mature and bear fruit unto him. It is time for us as the children of God to come further along into the truth about the manifold purpose for the incarnation of Christ. It is time to understand the phrase "for his name's sake."

Jesus prayed for us, saying to the Father, "Sanctify them by your truth. Your word is truth."[68] As we continue in the threefold revelation of truth, we can be certain that the Lord Jesus Christ will not be ashamed of us. Doesn't such an idea sound wonderful to you? We can do it! Let's do it, "for his name's sake"!

> For both He who sanctifies and those who are being sanctified are all of one, for which reason He is not ashamed to call them brethren, saying: …"Here am I and the children whom God has given me." We are for signs and wonders… from the LORD of hosts.
>
> Hebrews 2:11–13, Isaiah 8:18 (excerpts)

THE LITTLE CHILDREN
MAIN POINTS:

- As many as receive Christ become the children of God.
- Christ was manifested to take away our sins.
- A partial revelation of the purpose of the incarnation leads to a reduced Christian faith.
- The reduction of our Christian faith is tragic.
- All have sinned and come short of the glory of God.
- Bearing fruit unto God brings him glory.
- The immature believer, though a child of God whose sins are taken away, still remains in a state of unfruitfulness.
- Those who go on to maturity bear fruit and overcome the wicked one in this life.
- It is the "thorns" of this life that choke the word of God and hinder fruit bearing and the overcoming life.
- It is God's desire for Christ to bring many sons to glory (fruit bearing).
- Our sins were taken away, "for his name's sake."
- The truth sanctifies us.
- Jesus Christ is not ashamed to call the sanctified ones his brethren.

THE YOUNG MEN

My little children, for whom I labor in birth
again until Christ is formed in you.

Galatians 4:19

Finally, my brethren, be strong in the Lord and
in the power of His might.

Ephesians 6:10

The Eternal Word was manifest in the flesh to take
away our sins.[1] This is the first part of the threefold
cord of truth concerning the purpose for the incarnation. Far too many believers stop right here and go no
further with their Christian faith.

The revelation of the forgiveness of sins seems to be
the emphasis of what God has done for us. Without
minimizing the wonderful grace of God that enables us
to be born again and reconciled to him, we must look
deeper into the Scriptures and find another facet of the
revelation of the truth of the incarnation. If not, our
witness of God to the world is weak and uncertain. A
threefold revelation of truth provides certainty.[2]

The Scripture says, "I write to you, little children,
because your sins are forgiven you for His name's
sake."[3] While there is no conflict between the blessing
that God bestows upon us through the forgiveness of
sins and the phrase "for his name's sake," there certainly
is a distinction. The greatest story ever told is not only
about us and our salvation. It is about God and all that

he created, including us. Somehow, in the ages of time, the revelation of the honor, glory, and majesty of God's name has been distorted.

There can be little substantial dispute about it. It is obvious from the Scriptures that there was an angelic rebellion against the Creator God somewhere, somehow, some long time ago.[4] Since evil was already present in the garden of Eden (in the form of a serpent that deceived the first woman), there is evidence that such an angelic rebellion took place during some unspecified time before the creation of man.[5]

It is highly probable that God created man to be a part of the solution to the angelic rebellion. The Scripture boldly asks questions about man and provides the answers in Psalm 8:

> What is man that you are mindful of him, and the son of man that you visit him? For you have made him a little lower than the angels, and you have crowned him with glory and honor. You have made him to have dominion over the works of your hands; you have put all things under his feet.[6]

In the book of Hebrews, just before quoting these verses from Psalm 8, the Scripture makes it clear that the world to come will not be put in subjection to angels.[7] This indicates that it is probable that this present world was originally to be ruled for God by angels. After all, the devil is referred to as the "ruler of this world,"[8] "the god of this age,"[9] and the "prince of the power of the air."[10]

The Scripture also uses terms such as the "rulers of the darkness of this age," who are not of flesh and blood and "spiritual hosts of wickedness in the heavenly places."[11] The inference in such references is directed towards describing the inhabitants of the spiritual angelic world.

According to Psalm 8, which we have referred to, these spiritual beings apparently live on a higher dimension than man. Being spirits without bodies of flesh and blood, they are not subject to human mortality, the phenomenon of gravity and other "earthbound" limitations such as man is subject to. Hence, the psalmist noted that man has been made a little lower than the angels.[12]

However, since God has crowned man with glory and honor, and not angels, it is man who has been given dominion over the work of God's hands, all things being put under man's feet.[13] This is in agreement with the Genesis mandate given to man at his creation: "Then God said, 'Let Us make man in Our image, according to Our likeness; let them have dominion....'"[14]

This truth is also reinforced in Psalm 115 where it is written: "The heaven, even the heavens, are the LORD's; but the earth He has given to the children of men."[15] And again, for a third witness, this truth is made certain in the New Testament when the man Jesus Christ declared, "All authority has been given to Me in heaven and on earth. Go therefore and make disciples of all the nations...."[16]

It's as if Christ was saying, "I have come into this world as a man, taken away your sin, ended the rebellion in the spirit world that has brought evil to the earth, and I am now sending you in my name into all the world to enforce my victory!" The role that man is to play in this cosmic drama is greater than many immature Christians have realized. They seem to be satisfied in knowing that through Christ their sins have been taken away. This is such an important issue.

We know from New Testament revelation that we, God's people, are a chosen generation, a royal priesthood, a holy nation, his own special people who proclaim the praises of the One who called us out of darkness and into his marvelous light.[17] According to the revelation concerning man as revealed in Psalm 8, and the comments Jesus made about it in the New Testament, when we open our mouths and praise the Lord, we offer "perfected praise" with "ordained strength" that silences the enemy![18] This revelation is an awesome truth. Don't pass by it too quickly. Silencing the enemy is a major benefit provided by our victory in Christ. After all, the enemy's main weapon is the power of a lie.

We know that the first man, Adam, failed to fulfill the purpose for which God created him.[19] Adam was blessed by God to be fruitful, multiply, fill the earth, and subdue it, exercising Godly authority in the dominion of it.[20] Man was to rule the earth with the power and authority of the name of God Most High, thus the understanding that our sins were forgiven for his name's sake.

Although Adam failed, Jesus Christ, the Incarnate Word of God (called the last Adam and the second

Man[21]) completely fulfilled the plan and purpose of God.[22] He lived his life to honor the heavenly Father,[23] offered himself up as the payment for sin,[24] and was raised from the dead by the power of the Holy Spirit.[25] He offered praise to God in the midst of the great congregation.[26] His perfect praise with ordained strength to God silenced the enemy just as the psalmist said it would.

Jesus Christ totally disarmed the rebellious principalities and powers in the heavenly places (according to the eternal purpose of God[27]) and made a public spectacle of them, triumphing over them in it.[28] The book of Hebrews declares that Jesus became a man of flesh and blood, like the children of Adam, and through his death, destroyed (rendered entirely useless) he who had the power of death—the devil.[29] Take note and hold onto the word "destroyed." It will become a very important concept in the revelation of the purpose of the incarnation.

This is the Word of God. It is written, "Let all the angels of God worship Him [Jesus]."[30] All the angels, even the rebellious, must bow before him and confess that he is Lord to the glory of God the Father,[31] hence the concept of "for his name's sake." The angelic rebellion against God and the source of evil in the world has been conquered and destroyed by a man—the Man, Jesus Christ our Lord![32]

This is a revelation of the beginning of the second part of the reason that Christ was manifested in the flesh. Few Christians know it and fewer still live in the victory it has provided for us. In Christ and through the power of his blood, the sin issue is over *and* the devil has been defeated!

The blood of Christ purged our consciences from the dead works fostered in us by the evil works of the devil. Now we are free in and through Christ to serve the living God.[33] Once the blood has purged us, it is no longer necessary or expedient to remain in a paradigm of sin-consciousness![34]

Biblical maturity, translated as "perfection"[35] in the New Testament, can only be attained through the "perfect" work of the blood of Jesus. His blood was offered up to God as the payment for our sins—once for all.[36] Because of this "perfect" work, we have the opportunity as new creatures in Christ to be free from sin-consciousness by obtaining a renewed mind. Jesus Christ was manifested to take away our sins and our sin-consciousness!

This is why Paul admonished believers to present their bodies as living sacrifices, holy and acceptable to God.[37] As we acknowledge the "perfect" work of the blood of Jesus, we can be free from being conformed to the dead works of the sin-consciousness of this world and be transformed by the renewing of our minds![38] This renewed mind is nothing less than the mind of Christ![39]

Sin-consciousness and the subsequent overemphasis of the self-consciousness it produces are the results of man succumbing to the works of the devil. Remember in the garden of Eden God's question to Adam, "Who told you that you were naked [overly self-conscious and sin-conscious]?"[40] This self-consciousness arose as a result of sin as man disobeyed God and instead acted upon the lying works of the devil.

Thanks be to God for not leaving us in such a condition. Our former sins and subsequent sin-consciousness do not accompany us as we grow in maturity in this new life of Christ. In him, old things have passed way, all things have become new, and all things are of God.[41]

Jesus Christ did not only come to take away our sins. There is a second part of the revelation of the reason for the incarnation. It is written, "For this purpose the Son of God was manifested, that He might destroy the works of the devil."[42]

Do you know the second part of truth about the reason for the manifestation of Christ in the world? Do you live your life in the reality of the truth that Christ came not only to take away our sins but also to destroy the works of the devil?

Do you still succumb to sin-consciousness and self-consciousness and struggle in your daily life when your enemy, the devil and all his cohorts, have been totally defeated and disarmed? Christ destroyed the works of the devil and, believe it or not, actually rendered the devil and all his schemes against you entirely useless!

A closer look at the following three Scriptures will bring a certainty of this truth to reality in our lives. It is written in the epistle of Paul to the Colossian church:

> Having disarmed principalities and powers, He [Christ] made a public spectacle of them, triumphing over them in it.[43]

It is written in the book of Hebrews:

> Inasmuch then as the children have partaken of flesh and blood, He [Christ] Himself likewise shared in the same [the incarnation], that through [His own] death He might destroy him who had the power of death, that is, the devil.[44]

It is written in the second epistle of Paul to the Corinthian church:

> Now thanks be to God who always leads us in triumph in Christ, and through us diffuses the fragrance of His knowledge in every place.[45]

Let's look carefully now at these three verses. In the original Greek language, the word Paul used in his Colossian epistle that has been translated as "disarmed" actually means "to be divested" or "to get rid of something unwanted."[46] It is the opposite of "to invest," which means "to furnish or endow with positive qualities or value in order to obtain an increase or profit."[47] It is certain that the devil has been stripped, or divested, of all his weapons and power by the manifestation of Christ in the world!

It is also certain that the devil and his devices have been rendered "entirely useless" or made of "no effect" because Christ has taken upon himself the flesh and blood of the children of men and given his life for us. In the original Greek language of the Scripture, this is the meaning of the word translated "destroyed" in the verse we have identified from the book of Hebrews.[48]

The root of this word means "to be idle, inactive, and unemployed"![49] The devil is out of work! Or we could say, "No matter what the devil tries to do against us, it no longer works." The manifestation of Christ in the world has destroyed his works!

Think about it in simple everyday terms. When your car is in neutral, the motor may be running (idling), but the car is not going anywhere, is it? So it is with the devil and his vain attempts to continue to lie to those who have begun to mature in the revelation of truth concerning the manifestation of Christ in the world.

As we have recounted, the devil is silenced by the perfected praise of the saints. The psalmist said that the praise came out of the mouths of babes and children.[50] How much more will his schemes come to nothing when young men and young women in the kingdom of God begin to walk in the fuller revelation of truth!

This statement (not question) becomes a certainty for maturing believers as we realize the power in the triumph of Christ over the devil. In the original Greek language, the words translated "triumphing" in the Colossian epistle and "triumph" in the Corinthian epistle reveal a significant truth. The meaning of this word is "to make a noisy iambus, an acclamatory procession."[51] The word picture derived from the biblical concept of "triumph" is vivid and exact. Let me develop it for you. You will be thoroughly blessed!

In ancient times, it was common practice for military powers to demonstrate their total victory over their enemies by displaying their defeated foes in an open public exhibition. The conquerors would disarm the captured hostiles, strip them naked, and lead them through the streets in a celebratory parade.[52]

In this way the victims of the hostile enemy would be certain that the victory was complete and absolute. This parade was known as an "acclamatory procession." As the procession made its way through the streets, it would be preceded with loud applause and boisterous shouting. Such a commotion would serve to rally the beneficiaries of the victory and incite them to respond with the same acclamation to the good news of the defeat of their enemies.

The precise words used by Paul concerning this magnificent triumph are accurately described in the Greek dictionary as a "noisy iambus."[53] An "iamb" is a unit of timing used in verse, much like a marching cadence. It is a verse of one short syllable followed by a longer one, or an unaccented syllable followed by an accented one.[54]

Most of us are very familiar with this concept but just don't realize it. A noisy iamb would sound something like "TAH…..DAAH!" A noisy iambus would sound something like "TAH…..DAAH—TAH…..DAAH!"

Haven't you heard something like this on an occasion when a star, a celebrity, or a very important person shows up on the scene? They would be introduced with a "TAH…..DAAH!" which is to say, "Here he is!"

This acclamatory shout is also often used after the accomplishment of some great feat of valor. It's as if to say, "There, I did it!" It is a form of praise—perfected praise—in the sense of its recognition of something that has been done well. Many believe that the root of this expression comes from one of the ancient Hebrew words for praise—"tow-daw"![55] Need I say more? Our God truly is an awesome God! Jesus Christ was manifest to destroy the works of the devil and make a public spectacle of him!

The truth that Christ was manifest in flesh to destroy the works of the devil has tremendous implications for us. Some believers know this revelation of truth, but few live by it. There is a distinction to be found here in the level of growth experienced in the faith walk of a believer.

John wrote to "little children" because they knew that their sins were forgiven. He wrote to young men for a different reason. Young men know the second part of the answer to "why?" They know that Christ was manifest to destroy the works of the devil.

Young men also know that because the devil has been disarmed and his works destroyed by Christ that they too can be overcomers and more than conquerors "in this life."[56] John wrote, "I write to you, young men, because you have overcome the wicked one."[57] At this level of spiritual growth (knowing the second reason for the incarnation), the believer also enters into Christ's victory over the devil. Such a one joins in the acclamatory procession.

There can be no mistake about this revelation of truth. It is the second part of a threefold cord of excellence. Jesus clearly made this truth known to his disciples. Again, we refer to the words of Jesus after his resurrection. He commanded them, saying,

> All authority has been given to Me in heaven
> and on earth. Go therefore and make disciples
> of all the nations, baptizing them in the name
> of the Father and of the Son and of the Holy
> Spirit, teaching them to observe all things that
> I have commanded you; and lo, I am with you
> always, even to the end of the age.[58]

The disciples received the power of the Holy Spirit on the day of Pentecost and went out and did what he commanded.[59] A disciple is one who continues (abides) in God's Word, knowing the truth that makes them free.[60] To stop at the revelation that Christ was manifest to forgive our sins is to remain an immature child in the kingdom. Such a one remains immature, still in partial bondage to sin-consciousness and self-consciousness. They live in a world of "can't do" instead of "can do!"

A disciple of Christ continues in God's Word and walks in the truth of the revelation that Christ was also manifest to destroy the works of the devil. This is nothing less than the restoration of the Genesis mandate for man to exercise Godly dominion in all the earth. The disciples (young men and women) manifested this dominion and went out and continued to do the work that Jesus began to both do and teach.[61]

It is written, "And they went out and preached everywhere, the Lord working with them and confirming the word through the accompanying signs."[62] Think of it like this: because they filled out the blank check in his name—he signed it! He endorsed it! They cashed it! Do you get it?

Jesus had prayed that God the Father would sanctify these disciples by the truth (think threefold revelation) and keep them from all evil.[63] Think about it. Jesus prayed that his disciples would be kept from evil while they remained in this world.[64] Jesus also made it clear that his prayer was not limited to the twelve apostles or the seventy disciples that followed him a few thousand years ago.[65] He prayed to the Father saying, "I do not pray for these alone, but also for those who will believe in Me through their word."[66] As a disciple of Christ, that includes me. That can also include you. All that it takes for it to become a reality in your life is a step up from childhood into becoming a young man or woman of God.

This is not just a concept of truth but an actual lifestyle. John wrote: "I have written to you, young men, because you are strong, and the word of God abides in you, and you have overcome the wicked one."[67]

Notice, four times John says "you." Because Christ has destroyed the works of the devil, you can also overcome the wicked one. In this stage of spiritual growth, the emphasis shifts from Christ alone to Christ in you, the hope of glory![68]

According to the Scriptures, now—right now—we can thank God who always leads us in Christ's triumph and through our witness diffuses the fragrance of his knowledge in every place![69] Always means always! Now means now! Every place means every place!

In truth, the Scripture goes on to declare that in a profound way, our victorious faith walk is a continuation of the manifestation of Christ's destruction of the

works of the devil. The Scripture calls us "living epistles" of Christ, known and read by all men, written not
with ink, but by the spirit of the living God.[70] This is
a work of the same Spirit that raised Christ from the
dead in absolute victory and gives life to our mortal
bodies.[71]

Get ready now. This revelation of the second reason for the manifestation of Christ is leading us somewhere. The Scriptures that I am referencing are dancing
all around the third part of this excellent revelation of
truth. I pray that you are reading the scriptural references over and over. As you meditate on them day and
night, whatever you do will prosper.[72]

Can we really live the victorious Christian life as
overcoming young men and women in the kingdom of
God while we still live here and now in these mortal bodies? Yes, we can! The Word of God is absolutely clear.

By, through, and in Christ we have been given the
ministry of the glory of righteousness,[73] and the ministry of reconciliation.[74] We are, as I have already referenced, considered to be "living epistles;" a manifestation of the truth sent forth as ambassadors for Christ.[75]
However, life in this mortal body is not without its
challenges and struggles.

Such trials are to be considered the testing of our
faith which brings praise, honor, and glory at the revelation of Jesus Christ.[76] We are to be mature, not
just little children. We are to count our various trials
as joyful, knowing that such tests of our faith produce

patience in us. Patience has a perfect work by helping us to be mature and be complete, lacking nothing.[77]

It is through faith and patience working together that we come to inherit the promises of God.[78] Therefore, even in the face of the difficulties of this life, we do not lose heart.[79] We live for "his name's sake."

Young men and women know a secret about overcoming the wicked one. As recorded in the Bible, they know that "we have this treasure [the manifest Christ life] in earthen vessels that the excellence [threefold revelation of truth] may be of God and not of us."[80]

Now this is very important. The fullness of Christ's victory over evil is an unfolding revelation. While completely complete and already accomplished,[81] the full manifestation of this victory is a process. The mystery of Christ being formed in a corporate body of people has been going on for about two thousand years.[82] It is a work of glory! Knowing this truth brings certainty and stability to our daily lives.

In truth, the whole creation is waiting for the revealing of the sons (and daughters) of God.[83] As we mature and enter into the fellowship of not only the first part of the threefold reason for the manifestation of Christ but also the second and then the third, the entire creation itself will be delivered from the bondage of corruption caused by rebellion against God.[84] The sufferings of this present time are not worthy to be compared with the glory which shall be revealed in us![85]

Young men and women of God who are walking in the full revelation of the purpose of the manifestation of Christ know how this all works and comes together for good.[86] Please, continue to read and discover how you also can become strong and overcome the wicked one, in this life as well as the next! This is not fantasy or wishful thinking. This is where and how the rubber meets the road.

We must be fully aware that the treasure we are carrying (the Christ life being formed in us) is housed in an earthen vessel.[87] There is a sure and specific reason for this. This great story is not only about us. It is about God and all that he created, including us. It is all "for his name's sake."

The excellence of the power that works mightily in us must be manifested to clearly be of God and not of us.[88] It is the Christ in us that is the hope of the glory that reveals the fullness of God's eternal purpose. To reveal what is inside of something, there must be some way to get the inside out.

Therefore, as Christ is being formed in us we must accept that "We are hard-pressed on every side, yet not crushed; we are perplexed, but not in despair."[89] The apostle Paul said that we are "persecuted, but not forsaken; struck down, but not destroyed."[90] Why? Why must it be this way?

Paul revealed the secret of being changed from a child to a young man—of being changed "from glory to glory, just as by the Spirit of the Lord."[91] In this life, we carry about in our bodies the dying of the Lord Jesus.[92] This is the fellowship of his suffering—the price he paid for the forgiveness of our sins, and the sacrifice he made to obtain victory over the devil's works.

This we do so that we may know him and experience the power of his resurrection. When we carry the fellowship of this great price in our bodies, being conformed to his death[93], the actual life of Jesus is manifested in our very own lives.[94] Read it. "It is written."

What a glorious revelation of truth. It is this revelation that takes a little child in God's kingdom and grows him up to be a young man. There can be no doubt about this for the one who seeks to overcome evil in this life. The Scripture is absolutely clear. Paul said,

> For we who live [in the here and now] are always delivered to death for Jesus' sake [the fellowship of His sufferings], that the life of Jesus also may be manifested in our mortal flesh.[95]

It is essential for a young man or woman in God's kingdom to know that the victory over the devil's work only comes through death. It was through death that Jesus destroyed him who had the power of death; the devil.[96] This is precisely what the Scripture says.

The Scripture also says that "love is as strong as death"![97] Young men and women in God's kingdom are strong with the word of God abiding in them.[98] They are lovers. This is the source of overcoming the wicked one. Young men and women of God have learned that "'Greater love has no one than this, than to lay down one's life for his friends.'"[99]

To lay down one's life for others can mean to live for them. How could someone say "I would die for you" if they would not live for you? The first step to maturity once a little child has been born into the kingdom of

God is for them to realize that their sins are forgiven "for his name's sake."The biblical revelation is that their old life is dead and now their new life is hidden with Christ in God.[100] Now their new life is to be lived for him. How many actually know and live such a truth? This is Christianity 101!

The apostle Paul said,

> It is no longer I who live, but Christ lives in me; and the life which I now live in the flesh I live by faith in the Son of God who loved me and gave Himself for me.[101]

Read carefully, dear one—your spiritual growth depends upon it. Paul also said, "For he who has died has been freed from sin."[102]

Speaking of Christ (and those who live with him and for him), Paul declared that because of the resurrection, death no longer had dominion over him.[103] The death Christ died, he died to sin, once for all. The life he now lives, he lives to God.[104] This is our pattern for living. As he is, so are we in this world.[105]

We also are to consider ourselves to be dead to sin but alive to God in Jesus Christ our Lord.[106] This kind of living is a manifestation of our love for God. If we have been united together with Christ in the likeness of his death (to give one's life for another), certainly we also shall experience a newness of resurrection life here and now while we live in these mortal bodies.[107]

Such is the overcoming life of young men and women in the kingdom of God. Death works in them, but it brings life to others.[108] Through death, he who had the power of death has been rendered entirely useless.[109]

Young men and women are strong. They are overcomers. They do not lose heart even though the outward man (the mortal man) is perishing. They know the inward man is being renewed day by day.[110] They know that Jesus Christ, the Eternal Word manifest in the flesh, came to destroy the works of the devil as well as take away their sins.

Overcomers know that the light affliction experienced in this mortal life only lasts but a moment.[111] They know that the various trials of this life produce a genuine faith much more precious than any earthly possession. When tested by fire it is found to bring praise, honor, and glory at the revelation of Jesus Christ.[112]

Overcomers know that the fellowship of Christ's sufferings, the conformity to his death (love life), and the likeness of his resurrection are working for us (and in and through us) a far more exceeding and eternal weight of glory.[113]

Overcomers have learned the power and strength of the way of love—the giving of one's life for another. They see what little children do not see. They have continued in the word and are becoming free by their knowledge of the second part of the revelation of why Christ was manifested—to destroy the works of the devil through the way of love.

Overcomers do not look at the things which are seen but at the things which are not seen. They know that the things which are seen are temporary, but the things which are not seen are eternal.[114] They know that love endures forever.[115] Love outlasts everything. Dear reader, will you take another step with me into this life of love, this life of freely giving one's life for another, this life of living for another?

> Therefore, leaving the discussion of the elementary principles of Christ, let us go on to perfection [maturity], not laying again the foundation of repentance from dead works and of faith toward God, of the doctrine of baptisms, of laying on of hands, of resurrection of the dead, and of eternal judgment. And this we will do if God permits.
>
> Hebrews 6:1–3

THE YOUNG MEN

MAIN POINTS:

- Our sins are forgiven "for his name's sake."
- Somehow, in the ages of time, the name of God has been distorted by an angelic rebellion.
- Man, although a little lower than the angels, has been given dominion over the work of God's hands.
- Man's praise of God silences the angelic enemies.
- Through death, Jesus destroyed him who had the power of death; that is the devil.
- For this purpose, the Son of God was manifested, that he might destroy the works of the devil.
- Those in God's kingdom who mature beyond being a child and become young men and women also overcome the devil in this life.
- The full manifestation of this victory of the overcoming life and of freedom from sin-consciousness is a process.
- It is Christ in us (our mortal bodies) that is the hope of glory (that reveals the life of God in our mortal flesh).
- It is the love of God abiding in us (he died for us—we live for him) that gives us the power to live as overcomers in this life.

THE FATHERS

I write to you fathers because you have known Him who is from the beginning.

1 John 2:13a

And now, O Father, glorify Me together with Yourself, with the glory which I had with You before the world was. And the glory which You gave Me I have given them, that they may be one just as We are one.

John 17:5, 22

The word of the Lord is a fearful and glorious thing. While other glorious things pass away, it is eternal and abides forever.[1] How can man endure it?[2] In the days of the Old Covenant, the nation of Israel marveled that they could glimpse God's glory and hear his voice and yet still live.[3]

One of the most profound and essential communications between the Lord and Israel is found in the Old Testament book of Deuteronomy. It is called "The Shema."[4] It is a command given by God through Moses: "Hear, O Israel: The LORD our God, the LORD is one!"[5]

The context of this communication between God and his people is what has become known in both the Old and New Testaments as the "greatest commandment": "You shall love the LORD your God with all your heart, with all your soul and with all your strength."[6]

These words were to be known, fulfilled, and taught to all generations of Israel.[7]

In the Old Testament, the words of this great commandment immediately follow The Shema. In the New Testament, they are described along with the second great commandment, to love your neighbor as yourself, as being the essence of what all the Law and the Prophets are upheld by. The Shema and the two great commandments provide a threefold revelation of all that God requires of man. Through this revelation, we can be certain that our God is One in himself and that he desires for us to be one with him and one with one another.

The Shema is the expression of the unity of love: the Lord our God is one! This is a word for spiritual fathers. This word is not simply milk for newborn babes[8] or bread for overcoming young men.[9] It is strong meat for those who are coming to a full age of maturity.[10]

"One"—The Lord our God is one! As simple a statement as it seems to be, the profundity of it reaches back to "before the beginning." It reveals the very essence of the origin of all things that have been created by this great "One."

Jesus Christ our Lord came out of this "before the beginning" eternity and was manifested in our time and space world. Before the beginning, Jesus, the Word, was "one" with this great "One" identified in The Shema. It was a glorious love relationship between Father, Son, and Holy Spirit. During the final hours of his incarnation as a man, Jesus referred back to this relationship as he prayed:

> And now, O Father, glorify Me together with
> Yourself, with the glory which I had with You
> before the world was…for You loved me before
> the foundation of the world.[11]

Imagine with me what such a relationship may have been like. Out of this eternal relationship before time began, the plans for the creation of all things was decided. In omniscient foreknowledge of the necessity that would arise to redeem and restore what was to be lost through a rebellion, a plan was set in motion.

The plan would require that one of the members of the Godhead be sent into the world of time and space. The part of the Godhead that would be sent was called The Word, and then the plan began: "In the beginning, God created the heavens and the earth…and all the host of them."[12]

There are two places where "in the beginning" is recorded in the Scriptures; one in the Old Testament and one in the New. They do not signify two separate occasions, but the second record reveals one of the most significant revelations about the first. The opening statement made in the New Testament gospel of John declares, "In the beginning was the Word, and the Word was with God, and the Word was God. He was in the beginning with God."[13]

This is a reference to the pre-incarnate Son of God, Jesus, the Word. As previously planned in the Divine Counsel, there was an incarnation: "And the Word became flesh and dwelt among us, and we beheld His glory, the glory as of the only begotten of the Father, full of grace and truth."[14]

This incarnation of the Eternal Word would also come to be known as "The Lamb of God who takes away the sin of the world!"[15] The plan of God to accomplish this redemption and to begin the restoration of all that was lost was clearly decided before it began. The apostle Peter wrote,

> …knowing that you were not redeemed with corruptible things…but with the precious blood of Christ, as of a lamb without blemish and without spot. He indeed was foreordained before the foundation of the world, but was manifest in these last times for you . . .[16]

Yes, before we were even created, God had made the plan of redemption and restoration. As we have learned, he (God) chose us in him (Christ) before the foundation of the world, that we should be holy and without blame before him in love.[17]

The plan of God has not changed since the time it was agreed upon by the "One." A marvelous insight into this Divine Counsel was given through the prophet Isaiah. By divine revelation, he wrote this concerning the counsel of the "One":

> "Come near to Me, Hear this: I have not spoken in secret from the beginning; from the time that it was, I was there. And now the LORD GOD and His Spirit have sent Me."[18]

In this declaration, we get a glimpse into the mystery of the Godhead. The speaker appears to be the preincarnate Word. His announcement can be understood to explain that he is being sent into the world of time and space to redeem and restore as the Lamb of God. He declared that he was being sent by the Lord God and his Spirit. We can understand this to be a reference to the members of the "One" that we know as the Father and the Holy Spirit.

It is essential to note that in any good Bible translation, there is a footnote added at this place in Scripture. The footnote explains that the Hebrew verb describing the action is in the singular form of usage. From this, we can begin to understand more accurately The Shema concerning the "One" and the wonderful unity and glory of the plan of God that was agreed upon from "before the beginning."

Not only was Jesus Christ manifested in the world to take away our sins and to destroy the works of the devil, but also to make us one with God! To an immature believer and perhaps even to a young overcomer, this may sound like blasphemy and heresy. Yet, it is as scriptural as John 3:16!

Too many believers stumble over such a revelation. This stumbling is nothing new. To believe this truth and live it requires not only a new birth, but also a renewed mind, free from sin-consciousness. Even Jesus himself had to face the resistance to this revelation of truth.

When he declared to the religious leaders of his day that he and the Father were one, they took up stones to attempt to kill him.[19] Stoning was the capital punishment of that time for crimes that were so evil that only the death of the offender could satisfy justice.

Yes, this third part of the threefold revelation of the reason for the incarnation is meat for those coming to the full age of maturity. Through the magnificence of the Word of God and its precious promises and by the righteousness of Christ, we have been made to be partakers of the Divine Nature![20] I trust that you are reading God's Word!

Jesus Christ was manifest in this time and space world to make us one with God, in the same way that he is one with God. The glorious unity that the pre-incarnate eternal Word shared with the Father before the foundation of the world has been given to us through the complete work of the manifestation of Christ in the world! Jesus declared, "And the glory which You gave Me I have given them, that they may be one just as We are one."[21]

Through his birth, death, burial, resurrection, and ascension, Christ presents us to the Father declaring, "Here am I and the children whom God has given Me."[22] In Christ, we stand holy and without blame before him in love, just as the Father purposed before the foundation of the world.[23] The glorious unity of this holiness is the final part of the threefold cord of the revelation of why the Eternal Word became flesh and dwelt among us.

As we receive the blessing of the manifestation of Christ to take away our sins, we can stand as little children, blameless before God.[24] As we receive the blessing of the manifestation of Christ to destroy the works of the devil, we can stand as young men before him in love, overcoming the strength of death through the giving (living) of our lives wholly unto him.[25]

Finally, as we receive the blessing of the manifestation of Christ to make us one with God, we can stand as fathers, knowing him who is from the beginning—holy just as he is holy.[26] Gloriously sanctified by the truth,[27] we are sent into the world just as the Father sent the Incarnate Word into the world,[28] that the world may believe[29] and also be gathered together as one in Christ.[30]

This is the revelation of the mystery of the Father's will, according to his own good pleasure which he purposed in himself before the world was.[31] It is written in the book of Hebrews that without this holy unity, no one can see God.[32]

This is not my idea. It has been written as a prescription for us. How futile it is for immature Christians to attempt to be faithful and true witnesses of the glory, unity, and love of God without understanding The Shema and the two great commandments.

It is through the threefold purpose of the incarnation that man can behold (and be one with) the glory of God. It is written, "And the Word became flesh and dwelt among us, and we beheld His glory, the glory as of the only begotten of the Father, full of grace and truth."[33]

The Scripture continues, "No one has seen God at anytime. The only begotten Son, who is in the bosom of the Father, He has declared Him."[34] Jesus Christ, the Incarnate Word, declares the name of God in the midst of the great congregation of the family of God.[35] He is not ashamed to call us the Father's own, for both he who sanctifies (Jesus) and those who are being sanctified are all of one (the Father).[36]

Jesus Christ our Lord was manifest to bring many sons to glory![37] It is the same glory that he shared with the Father from the beginning, before the world was.[38] This is the truth concerning the incarnation. Jesus said to Pilate, "'For this cause I was born, and for this cause I have come into the world, that I should bear witness to the truth.'"[39] Even as a child, Jesus said to his earthly parents, "Did you not know that I must be about My Father's business?"[40]

The truth is that Jesus came into the world to do the will and work of the Father and glorify Him on earth.[41] When Jesus came into the world, he said, "'Behold, I have come—In the volume of the book it is written of Me—To do Your will, O God.'"[42] It is by that will that we have been sanctified and become one with God.[43]

Jesus declared to the multitudes, "For I have come down from heaven, not to do My own will, but the will of Him who sent Me.'"[44] As Jesus neared the conclusion of fulfilling the Father's will of reconciling the world to himself through the incarnation, he made it very clear why he had come. Not only did he come to take away our sins and to destroy the works of the devil, he also came to glorify the Father and make us one with him. Oh, that God's people would return to the Bible!

As the end of his earth life neared, Jesus was very troubled in his soul.[45] He was suffering the heavy weight of taking away our sins and destroying the works of the devil. It was to become so exceedingly sorrowful and agonizing that his sweat became like great drops of blood.[46]

It was in moments like these that Jesus sustained and strengthened himself by fixing his eyes on the final part of the purpose of his manifestation. He prayed to the Father saying,

> Now My soul is troubled, and what shall I say? 'Father, save Me from this hour'? But for this purpose I came to this hour. Father glorify Your name.[47]

Again Jesus prayed, saying,

> Father, the hour has come. Glorify Your Son, that Your Son also may glorify You. I have glorified You on the earth. I have finished the work [threefold] which you have given Me to do. And now, O Father, glorify Me together with Yourself, with the glory which I had with You before the world was.[48]

Dear reader, it is time for the church to mature. Thank God that his little children know that Jesus came to take away our sins. It is through such knowledge that we know we are born of God and that he is our heavenly Father. But that is not enough truth to change us sufficiently to change the world. It is only the first part of the threefold reason for the incarnation of the Word.

The church must come to know that Jesus also came to destroy the works of the devil. The sin issue is over. We are to be strong in the Lord and the power of his might, overcoming the wicked one ourselves, in this life. Yet, even that is not enough truth to change the world.

Jesus Christ also came into the world to make us one with God. This revelation of truth is a threefold cord that is not easily broken.[49] Has not God written to us excellent (threefold) things that we may know the truth for certain and have answers that are true for those who ask us?[50] It is only by a living demonstration of the threefold truth of the incarnation that the world will believe the Father truly sent the Son.[51]

We begin our new life as children and then grow into adulthood. Then it is through the revelation of the eternal purpose of God accomplished through the incarnation of Christ Jesus our Lord, that we become fathers in the faith, knowing him who is from the beginning.[52] This wonderful life experience is all about the "One" (Father, Son, and Holy Spirit) and his glory from eternity past to eternity future. As children of God, we are to be included in the "one" and his glory.

It is only as we become fathers in the faith that we can be fruitful and multiply, bearing fruit that remains.[53] It is the fathering spirit—knowing him who is from the beginning and being one with him in glory that gives life to others. Let me explain.

Jesus said,

> Most assuredly [with threefold certainty], I say to you, he who believes in Me, the works that I do [glorifying the Father] he will do also; and greater works than these he will do, because I go to My Father.[54]

Remember, in the same way as the Father sent Jesus into the world, he has also sent us.[55] We were chosen in Christ before the foundation of the world, that we should be holy and without blame before him in love.[56]

Jesus made it clear. He proclaimed that we did not choose him but he chose us. Not only did he choose us, but according to the eternal purpose, he appointed us that we should go and bear fruit. He declared that the fruit we bear should remain—be eternal.[57]

Jesus indicated that in so doing, we would be entering with him into the ultimate part of the purpose of the incarnation. He said, "By this is my Father glorified, that you bear much fruit..."[58] This is nothing less than our oneness with the One who is from the beginning. This is eternal life—past, present, and future. Only life can beget life.

The knowledge of him who is from the beginning is the level of maturity that the church must grow into in order for the world to believe in the incarnation and experience the threefold accomplishment of the manifestation of God in the flesh. They must have an opportunity to read a living epistle, to see a faithful and true witness, and to touch and handle the Word of life.

This is the message which the fathers in the faith have heard and still declare. Please read slowly and carefully the words of the apostle John:

> That which was from the beginning, which we have heard, which we have seen with our eyes, which we have looked upon, and our hands have handled, concerning the Word of life— the life was manifested, and we have seen, and

> bear witness, and declare to you that eternal life
> which was with the Father and was manifested
> to us—that which we have seen and heard we
> declare to you, that you also may have fellow-
> ship with us; and truly our fellowship is with
> the Father and with His Son Jesus Christ. And
> these things we write to you that your joy may
> be full.[59]

Herein do we find the excellence, the certainty of truth that will change the world. It is not just the knowledge of the forgiveness of sins. It is not just the knowledge of the destruction of the works of the devil. It is the knowledge and fellowship of the love of Father God, the grace of our Lord Jesus Christ and the communion of the Holy Spirit.[60]

Again, we look at the Old Testament prophecy of Isaiah that foreshadowed this glorious threefold unity of the Father, Son, and Holy Spirit into which we have been invited to share. In prophetic utterance before the incarnation, the Eternal Word (pre-incarnate Jesus) declared,

> Come near to Me, hear this: I have not spoken
> in secret from the beginning; From the time
> that it was, I was there. And now the Lord God
> and His Spirit have sent Me.[61]

This is the witness of God to man.[62] There are three who bear witness in heaven—the Father, the Word, and the Holy Spirit—and these three are one.[63] This is the glorious unity that has been provided for us through the threefold manifestation of Christ in the world.

This is the glory coming to the church. As we mature beyond being little children and young men and grow into fatherhood, we can pray as Jesus prayed. Our prayer must become like his prayer. It is time for the fathers to pray such a prayer as this:

> Our Father, glorify your church, the Body of Christ, that we may glorify you. Glorify us with the same glory that you shared with your Son and your Spirit before the world was. May we all be one.
>
> Help us mature that the world may know that you love them the same way you love us. May we learn to love you with all of our hearts, all of our souls, and all of our might. May we also learn to love our neighbors the way we love ourselves. May Christ live in us as a continuing incarnation of the Eternal Word, in the body that has been prepared for him.[64]

Those who pray in this manner can become fathers who find the manifestation of eternal life in him who is from the beginning. Jesus defined eternal life for us. Praying to the Father, he said, "And this is eternal life, that they may know You, the only true God, and Jesus Christ whom You have sent."[65]

The psalmist David glimpsed this eternal life and the glorious unity of the family of God. He said, "Behold, how good and pleasant it is for brethren to dwell together in unity! For there the LORD commanded the blessing—life forevermore."[66]

We have been called to the fellowship of God's Son, Jesus Christ our Lord.[67] He is our forerunner, having entered the Presence behind the veil.[68] He is appearing now in the presence of God for us.[69] We could say that we are appearing now in the presence of people for him.[70]

We are on a mission from heaven—ambassadors for Christ in this world.[71] We have been sent from his presence, where there is fullness of joy,[72] with a message to mankind. We declare as the heavenly host did at the incarnation, "Glory to God in the highest, and on earth peace, goodwill toward men!"[73]

Ours is a message of good tidings of great joy which is for all people—whoever will believe.[74] The apostle Peter said that this genuine faith proclaims a message of joy that is unspeakable and full of glory.[75] This is why someone has said, "Preach the good news always—use words when necessary."[76] It is our lifestyle that speaks the loudest.

Peter indicated that by experiencing this inexpressible joy that is full of glory (our participation in the eternal oneness of our God), we receive something special. He wrote, "...receiving the end of your faith—the salvation of your souls."[77]

What good news! It becomes even greater when you read the Scriptures carefully. In some cases, the translators have added words to the ancient manuscripts in an attempt to better explain their meaning. Sometimes, this is good and helpful—sometimes, it is not so.

The ancient text of Peter's epistle does not include the word "your" in the referenced verse. The translators added it. That is why in a good translation the word is in italics. Peter actually wrote, "...receiving the end of your faith—the salvation of souls."[78]

In light of this, we could say that little children thank God for the salvation of their own souls. Young men are strong and do something about the salvation of the souls of others. Fathers, who know him who is from the beginning, manifest the glory of God so that all those souls who ask can be certain of the truth—knowing that from the beginning, before the foundation of everything, "God so loved the world...."[79]

It is time to grow up. There is one body and one Spirit, one hope of calling, one Lord, one faith, one baptism; one God and Father of all, who is above all, and through all, and in all who believe.[80] This is the final part of the threefold cord of why Christ was manifested.

It is the glorious unity of the Spirit in the bond of peace between God and man.[81] We should no longer be (little) children, tossed to and fro and carried about with every wind of doctrine. Speaking the truth in love, we are to grow up (as young men and fathers) in all things into him who is the head (of the body)—Christ (the Incarnate Word of God).[82]

The apostle Paul is an example of being a father in the faith. In the context of being stewards of these mysteries of God, Paul addressed the immaturity found in the Corinthian church and wrote this:

> I do not write these things to shame you, but as my beloved children I warn you. For though you might have ten thousand instructors in Christ, yet you do not have many fathers; for

in Christ Jesus I have begotten you through the
gospel. Therefore I urge you, imitate me.[83]

These words of Paul are rich with meaning. The
church needs more than instructional teaching. The
church needs fathers who are living examples that provide a certain manifestation of the new life in Christ.
When Paul wrote "imitate me," he was saying something deeper than a casual observance reveals.

Paul's usage of the Greek work that is translated as
"imitate" in the NKJV of our Bible, really means to live
or act out, not only in word or with words, but also in
deed.[84] The emphasis of the word insists on an active
faith, not just a mental apprehension.

The root of the word chosen by Paul is the derivative
of our English word "mime" which means to commu-
nicate by acting out. By the context of his words, Paul
was clearly referring to the active influence that a father
has over a son.

We often use the term "like father, like son." We also
often hear negligent, immature fathers say to their sons,
"Do as I say, not as I do." What Paul is really saying is,
"Do as I say, just as I also do!"

It is this type of father to son relationship that is
lacking in much of today's church just as it was in
Paul's day. Paul spoke to the believers in Corinth as
a father, not simply as an instructor. This concept is
essential for us to grasp and to begin to live out in our
own relationships.

While instruction from teachers is good and scriptural,[85] it is insufficient to bring believers to maturity. The biblical pattern can be found in the Old

Testament in the statement of Hezekiah. After his life was miraculously extended by the power and grace of God, Hezekiah wrote, "The living, the living man, he shall praise you, as I do this day; the father shall make known your truth to the children."[86]

A second Old Testament witness to this superior pattern of instructing and imparting truth to the younger ones among us is found in the Psalms where the psalmist Asaph wrote,

> We have heard and known the parables and mysteries of old. Our fathers have told us. They did not hide them from the children. They told the generation to come about the praises of the LORD and the wonderful works he has done. For God established it as a testimony and law among us. He commanded our fathers to make the truth known to the children who would be born, even the generation to come, that they would arise and declare these things to their children also.[87]

And so, we find Paul in good standing in communicating truth to the church in Corinth as a father rather than as a teacher. Paul addressed those that he had "begotten" through the gospel. It is the role of the father to beget.

There is a simple way to express the progression of maturity in the life of a newborn believer in Christ. Once someone believes in their heart unto righteousness and confesses Christ with their mouth unto salvation, they receive him and become a child of God.[88] Each individual must do this on their own. No one can have this experience on someone else's coattails or say-so.

However, having now entered into the family of God, he soon discovers that he is no longer alone. Once he believes unto salvation he also "belongs." This can be likened to the state of childhood experienced by someone who has come to the knowledge that Jesus Christ was manifested to take away their sins. Such a one is now numbered among the newborns of God and finds that he has brothers and sisters like himself.

Once this newborn begins to grow in the Word, drinking not only of its pure milk[89] but also taking nourishment of the Word as bread[90] as one who belongs, he begins to "behave." This can be likened to the state of young adulthood experienced by someone who has come to the knowledge that Christ was manifested to take away his sins and to destroy the works of the devil.

The Word becomes true in such a one's life just as it is written of young men; they "overcome the wicked one and are strong, having the Word abide in them."[91] Those that believe—belong. Those that belong—behave. There is a maturing from childhood to young adulthood.

As we follow the progression of maturity in the life of a believer, there is a final step. It requires that one be mature enough to "really" teach others also, not just in word but also in deed. It is called the partaking of meat for those who are of full age.[92]

One who believes belongs. One who belongs behaves. One who behaves "begets." The final step of adulthood should be the "begetting" of others. This is a description of a mature father (or mother) who knows that Jesus was manifested in the flesh to make us one with God. This is why Paul could address those that he had begotten in the faith as his spiritual children. He was a father, knowing him who is from the beginning.

Much of what we see in today's church world is the flawed "begetting" of those born into God's kingdom with "birth defects" that prevent them from growing into full stature in Christ. No one has led them into a revelation of truth beyond knowing that their sins were taken away.

The truth revealed in The Shema and the two great commandments must be lived out by the Body of Christ in the flesh. It takes maturity, but we can and must do it. To love God and live for him with all of our being is to be one with him. To love others in the same way is to demonstrate the reality of the original intention of God in creating, redeeming, and restoring all that was lost.

It is high time for the church to awake out of sleep for truly our salvation is nearer than when we first believed.[93] It's time for fathers to speak the truth in love that we may grow up in all things into him who is the head of the Body—Jesus Christ![94]

God's divine power has given to us all things that pertain to life and godliness (God-likeness) through the knowledge of Christ.[95] Through exceedingly great and precious promises given to us by Christ we have indeed become partakers (part-takers) of the Divine Nature. This is not heresy. This is biblical truth.[96] Let

us, each one of us, decide to do our part. Yes? Amen?
Yes! Amen!

> For all the promises of God in Him are Yes, and
> in Him Amen, to the glory of God through us.
>
> 2 Corinthians 1:20

THE FATHERS
MAIN POINTS:

- According to The Shema, the Lord our God is One.
- The Scripture reveals the Godhead as the Father, the Word, and the Spirit.
- It is the Word that has come into the world and become flesh.
- The completed work of the incarnation of the Word restores mankind's glorious unity with God.
- Through Christ, "born-again" believers partake of God's Divine Nature.
- Those who come to the maturity of being "fathers" in the faith live in this glorious unity that was experienced by the Godhead before the world was.
- Jesus Christ is bringing many sons to the glory of oneness with God.
- God the Father is glorified as his children mature and bear fruit that remains.
- It is time for the church to pray in the manner that Jesus prayed, saying, "Glorify us with the glory you shared with the Eternal Word and the Spirit, that as one we may glorify you."

- The "end of our faith" leads to the saving of souls.
- The church needs "fathers" to be living examples of this level of growth and maturity.
- It is the "fathers" that make the truth known to the children.
- "Fathers" beget others in the faith who are free from birth defects.

THE JOURNEY

...till we all come to the unity of the faith and of the knowledge of the Son of God, to a perfect man, to the measure of the stature of the fullness of Christ

Ephesians 4:13

Therefore you shall be perfect, just as your Father in heaven is perfect.

Matthew 5:48

Almost anyone, just about everyone, can be engaged into discussing the question "Is there life after death?" It certainly is an interesting question. Finding an answer that "one can live with" is important. However, since I am alive and not dead, I am more interested in declaring, "There is life after birth!"

Now that I find myself alive, not just with a biological experience but with a vibrant new life in Christ, I am more interested in the process of fulfilling the purpose for which I have been given this new life than I am in the afterlife. As a partaker (part-taker) of the Divine Nature I want to live this life to its fullest and reach the destination that the "One" who has given me this life intends for me to reach.

As referenced in the Scripture that opens this chapter, we could understand the intended destination, as described by the apostle Paul, to be "a perfect man in the measure of the stature of Christ's fullness."[1] It is recorded in the gospels that Jesus used the same word as Paul did, teaching that we can become "perfect" to the same degree as our heavenly Father is.[2]

We should not stumble at the word "perfect"! In the Greek language that the New Testament Scripture is written in, it simply means "complete" or we could also say "mature."[3] I will develop this concept as you read on.

We should think of this "completeness" as the reaching of a desired destination at the end of a planned journey. We could also think of "maturity" as growing from infancy to a *full* stature of adulthood. I will use both analogies to help bring understanding as we proceed.

Let's look at the concept of a journey. It is the means of fulfilling the intention to get from "here" to "there." We could say it is the process we use to get from "where we are" to "where we want to be." Therefore, a journey is a process of steps that produce an "arrival" out of a "departure."

According to the finished work of the cross,[4] God has delivered us from the power of darkness and translated us into the kingdom of the Son of his love.[5] It is also written that he has called us out of darkness into his marvelous light.[6]

We should embrace the biblical concept of "out of" and "into." This pattern has always been used by God. It is vividly portrayed in the Old Testament as well as in the New. God led the captive nation of Israel "out of" Egyptian bondage and "into" the Promised Land.

However, getting "out of" and "into" is not the intended end of the matter. Going "on in" or "on to" has always been the plan of God. The book of Hebrews says it like this: "Let us go on to perfection…And this we will do if God permits."[7] I would like you to consider that if you have read this far, you have in effect received a "permit" from God to continue on his pre-planned journey into maturity. As we continue together, I would like to apply a principle of "journey wisdom," a kind of "map reading" so that we are properly prepared to understand what lies between the "here" and the "there" of our journey.

As always, the word of God is the best road map that we can use. It is a light unto our path and a lamp unto our feet.[8] In the ninth chapter of Luke, Jesus sent his disciples out to preach the kingdom of God, to heal the sick, and to cure all diseases.[9] Before he sent them out "into" and "on in," he made sure that they were first "out of" the weak and powerless state of fallen man. He gave them power and authority to fulfill their assignment before they began the journey.

As we read, it will be wise to apply to our own journey the instructions given by Jesus to those he sent "out of," into," and "on in." He said to them, "Take nothing for the journey, neither staffs nor bag nor bread nor money; and do not have two tunics apiece."[10]

Applying this command to what you are reading, it would be wise to lay aside (at least temporarily) any staffs (mindsets) that may have previously been used to support your belief system concerning "life after birth" issues. It would also be wise to lay aside (at least temporarily) any other life support systems (bag, bread, money, tunics) that may hinder the revelation of and the proper interpretation of the planned travel route.

Sometimes, what we already know or think we know about an issue dims our perception of something new when it is presented to us. In our generation, there is much teaching concerning the Scriptures, but much of it is not the true message that God is communicating to us.

As the founding and senior pastor of what has been and still is after twenty-seven years considered to be a "present truth"[11] church, I think it correct to say that there are some, but few indeed, among us that are actually aware of this journey, let alone making it. So much of Christendom, especially in our nation, has reduced God's message to us to be concerned primarily with the issue of life after death, at the expense of life after birth.

Do not mistake my statements as being pessimistic or critical. I believe with all my heart that the church is about to experience God's "warp speed" acceleration to take us where none of us have gone before.

I have been told a story about a present day minister who a few years ago was experiencing this type of acceleration on his own journey and was "drafting" many others in his energy to seek and find God. He was asked, "How did this happen to you? It seems as if it happened overnight. Did it?"

It has been said that he so wisely and succinctly answered, "Yes, but it was a long night!"[12] Oh yeah! With an optimistic and encouraging spirit, I prophecy to you, "Morning comes! The Bright and Morning Star is arising with healing in his wings. The messenger of the covenant will suddenly come to his people and we shall take a giant step on our journey into maturity!"[13]

There really is a journey to embark on in this "life after birth." It will take us from infancy through the varying stages of growth to our final destination—perfection, completeness, maturity in Christ. The apostle John, himself maturing as a father in the faith, recognized this truth and wrote, "I have no greater joy than to hear that my children walk in truth."[14] Our journey is simply a walk in truth.

John's fatherly instruction and impartation to his children in the faith concerning the brethren and even strangers echoed and mirrored his own maturity. He wrote, "If you send them forward on their journey in a manner worthy of God, you will do well."[15] John recognized that those who embark on the journey travel not only for themselves but also for Christ. He also wrote, "…they went forth for His name's sake."[16]

This is my intention. I would like to help you along on the journey. If you can understand, helping you also helps me as I expand my own heart and renew my own mind by writing about these things. I am writing in faith, believing that these words will bring edification.

Let me describe the road map. I'm going to imagine it to be the journey from the Alpha to the Omega, titles that are ascribed to the author and finisher of our planned faith journey.[17] This journey must take us through what I will call "The Lost World." It is the space of time found between the life we live after being born again and the day we die and enter the "afterlife."

I call it lost because so few really find it. It is only found through what Jesus called "the straight gate and the narrow way" that leads to life.[18] In order to map this journey out accurately, it will be necessary to be a little more technical and studious in handling the Word of God.

I will systematically lay the journey out by listing some Greek words as used in the New Testament along with their fuller meanings in our own language. After I have done so, it will become apparent that these words reveal a series of sequential steps that lead to a preplanned destination. Then I will provide scriptural references for each word that will demonstrate the validity, value, and revealed truth of the word study.

The Greek words and their fuller meanings are:

- Teknon: a born one, infant.[19]
- Nepios: a toddler with "no words."[20]
- Paidion: a child under discipline and training.[21]
- Neaniskos: a youthful regenerated new man.[22]
- Huios: a full grown son (or daughter).[23]
- Pater: an imparter of life, a parent.[24]
- Teleios: a perfect, mature, full grown, complete adult.[25]

I think it is already obvious when considering the fuller meaning of these Greek New Testament words that they reveal and describe a journey. The sequence of steps takes a person "out of" infancy and "into" what I defined as "The Lost World." This part of the journey is not a rest stop or the final destination. There is to be no exit ramp found in The Lost World. It is not a bus stop or a train station either. The traveler is to go "on in" or "on to" the final destination of maturity, passing through the various stages of personal growth.

Readers of the Bible may not realize this at first (or at all) because in many cases (especially in the earlier stages of the journey), the translators made no distinction between the words found in the ancient manuscripts. Instead, they used words such as "child," "children," or "son" in translation, words which in our own English language can be interpreted to be synonymous.

Because of this, a casual reader does not recognize the importance of a fuller understanding of what the message of the Scripture really is. The various writers, inspired by God, chose very specific Greek words that in fact make the steps and the process of the journey clear.

Now is an appropriate time to go to work. Though tedious, our exegesis of particular Scripture verses will yield a gold mine of reward. Remember, "It is the glory of God to conceal a matter, but the glory of kings is to search out a matter."[26]

You will experience a "royal" blessing as truth is revealed through diligent searching. The apostle Paul, with a fathering spirit, wrote to Timothy, his son in the faith, admonishing him to "study to show yourself approved to God, a worker who does not need to be ashamed, rightly dividing the word of truth."[27]

Make no mistake about it. Not only is there a blessing waiting for you on this journey "on in" to your life after birth but also for your children—both natural and spiritual. The Scripture declares:

> The secret things belong to the LORD our God, but those things which are revealed belong to us and to our children forever, that we may do

all the words of this law [take all the steps of the journey].[28]

Let's go to work. John 1:12 actually reads like this: "But as many as received Him, to them He gave the right to become 'born ones, infants' [teknon] of God, even to those who believe in His name." This Scripture reveals the beginning of the journey when one is "born again" and becomes a new creature in Christ.[29] The born one is just an infant. Think about newborn babes. They are alive—fully alive—but only in a state of infancy. Infancy in Christ is not the final destination of our journey. Let's take another step. We find that Ephesians 4:14–15 actually reads:

> ...we should no longer be "toddlers, children who cannot speak" [nepios], tossed to and fro and carried about with every wind of doctrine, by the trickery of men, in the cunning craftiness by which they lie in wait to deceive, but, speaking the truth in love, may grow up in all things into him who is the head—Christ.

This Scripture reveals the part of the journey after leaving infancy and is where so many Christians get stuck. The term "nepios" does not describe a newborn but one who is a toddler who hasn't learned to speak yet. It is a compound word made up of a negative particle and the root of "to speak." Its real meaning is to be an "immature" Christian with "no words." This is why the verses exhort such a one to "speak truth and grow up."

To remain at this level of growth or to stay at this place of "no words" is tragic. First of all, we are called to be witnesses and to testify to the world of the gospel of the kingdom of God, which includes having the ability to speak.[30] A worse tragedy occurs when a toddler who cannot speak (having no words) attempts to, and his words come out only in a "goo-goo" or "ga-ga" language and is misunderstood by those he is speaking to.

That type of language is fine at home and in the playpen (for a season) and all "born ones" should reach this stage of growth. But it is tragic to speak of the mysteries of Christ and his kingdom in this manner when we are out in the world of unsaved and dying people! It causes them to mock our faith.

Usually, "nepios" children are not fully "potty trained." Think about it. Much of the Christian testimony we present to our culture comes from a playpen full of nonsense words that are carried by the foul odor of an unchanged diaper!

Am I being too harsh? I think not. I hope you can laugh and cry with me. Unfortunately, too many of the leaders in much of the church are also stuck at this stage of the journey. Their diapers are full of "every wind of doctrine." They are continually "tossed to and fro" from the arms of one cultural fad to another. The church and the culture would be much better off if those with "no words" closed their mouths until they reached the next stage of the journey and obtained some!

The next step on the journey requires more training. 1 John 2:13b actually reads: "I write to you little 'disciplined and trained ones' [paidion] because you have known the Father." In this verse, John is addressing those children of God who have outgrown the toddler stage and have come under the discipline and training of their parents. They are no longer in a playpen with dirty diapers and no words.

Under parental guidance and supervision, they are experiencing the next part of the journey into maturity. The word "paidion" comes from the root word meaning "to hit." This concept is indicative of the wisdom of the Proverbs which states, "He who spares his rod hates his son, but he who loves him disciplines him promptly."[31]

Again, the wisdom of Proverbs describes this stage of life by the admonition that says:

> Do not withhold correction from a child, for if you beat him with a rod, he will not die. You shall beat him with a rod, and deliver his soul from hell.[32]

Dear reader, this is the wisdom of God, not a policy of child abuse! Our homes and our churches are full of undisciplined children because of the many lies introduced by our culture concerning the raising of our children. We have allowed the philosophy of secular humanists to dictate to us about how to treat our children.

Please brace yourself. Because we have succumbed to the lies of the wicked and ignored the truth of the word of God, we are raising up a generation of "bastards!" Or we could say unsuccessfully trying to raise them in the faith. Hebrews 12:8 is very clear about this as it says, "But if you are without chastening, of which all [sons] have become partakers, then you are illegitimate and not sons.

The word "chastening" is the Greek word "paideia" meaning "disciplinary correction"[33] and is derived from the same root as "paidion." Coming to and passing through this stage of the journey is absolutely essential for the children of God.

Again, the Book of Proverbs is replete with the wisdom of discipline. It is written:

> Foolishness is bound up in the heart of a child; the rod of correction will drive it far from him.[34] Blows that hurt cleanse away evil, as do stripes the inner depths of the heart.[35] Faithful are the wounds of a friend, but the kisses of an enemy are deceitful.[36]

Let's continue with our study of the journey. The next step is a huge one. Excerpts from 1 John 2:13–14 state:

> I write to you "youthful, regenerated new men" [neaniskos] because you have overcome the wicked one. I have written to you "youthful, regenerated new men" because you are strong, and the word of God abides in you, and you have overcome the wicked one.

Now we are getting somewhere on our journey. No longer infants, no longer toddlers with no words, and no longer needing strict discipline (already having been trained by it) at this stage of maturity, the child of God is not only experiencing Christ's victory but actually enforcing it!

At this stage of maturity, the child of God begins to really understand and see what God sees. The prophecy of Joel begins to be a reality in their lives. Joel prophesied, "Your young men [neaniskos] shall see visions."[37] Seeing visions denotes the ability to discern the invisible things that go on in the spirit world.[38]

Also, at this stage of maturity, the words, the testimony, and the witness of the child of God become substantial and weighty. A "neaniskos" can render decisions and judgments that confirm or overrule the actions of others.

Although the stoning of the martyr Stephen is set in a negative context, insight into the stature of a "neaniskos" can be gleaned from it. Stephen was accused of blasphemy for the testimony of his faith.[39] His accusers ran at him, dragged him out of the city, and stoned him. Those who witnessed this laid their garments down at the feet of a "young man" named Saul[40] (he later became the apostle Paul) who was standing by and observing the angry crowd. This might have been because of his stature in the community and it appears to have been in his power to stop them.

The ensuing verses indicate that he gave them the "nod" and consented to Stephen's death.[41] Yes, the words "young man" are from the Greek word "neanias" meaning "a man of stature" and comes from the same root as "neaniskos"![42]

In a positive context, it would be wonderful if the church was filled with children of God who were at this stage of maturity on the journey! So much nonsense goes on in "church life" with so few mature enough to stand and overrule it.

We have not yet completed our description of the journey. There are other great steps to be taken so let's keep going. A paraphrased compilation of Galatians 4:1–7 actually reads:

> Now I say that the heir, as long as he is a "toddler," a child who cannot speak [nepios], does not differ at all from a slave, though he is master of all, but is under guardians [overturners; Greek word "epitropos"[43]] and stewards [household managers; Greek word "oikonomos"[44]] until the time appointed by the father. Even so we, when we were "toddlers," children who could not speak, were in bondage [to the world]…were redeemed…that we might receive the adoption—placement as "full grown sons" [huiothesia; from huios[45]]. And because you are "full grown sons" [huios], God has sent forth the Spirit of his "full grown son" into your hearts, crying out, "Abba, Father!" Therefore you are no longer a slave but a "full grown son," and if a "full grown son," then an heir of God, through Christ.

It is as clear as can be. A child of God does not, and cannot, become an heir of God until he reaches the stage of maturity as a full grown son. This is why so much that is done "in the name of Jesus" does not actually make a difference in people's lives. Jesus never signs the check! So many act before being adopted or placed in a position of authority.

Authorization to use Christ's name must first come from the Father. It is the "huiothesis," the recognition and placement as a son that comes only from the Father through his Son Jesus that empowers a child of God to act fully in the name of the Lord.

I trust that you are seeing the importance of recognizing the steps of the journey and embarking on it. The word of God explained in the preceding chapters comes alive once you embark on the journey. Let's be aggressive about this. There is still more ground to cover; there is much further to go. All of these truths must be considered in both an individual light and a corporate "Body of Christ" light. I trust that you are thinking in this way.

There are at least two more steps to take on the journey. 1 Corinthians 4:15 says:

> For though you might have ten thousand instructors in Christ, yet you do not have many "imparters of life" [paters]; for in Christ Jesus I have begotten [to procreate, to generate; Greek word "gennao"[46]] you through the gospel.

This Greek word, "gennao," is from the same root from which we derive our English words genesis, gene, and generation and speaks of fatherhood. Only those who have life can beget life. The covenant and blessings of God were always intended to be generational. Without those in the kingdom who can "impart" and "pass on" life, the church and the world suffer.

One of our culture's main problems can be summed up in the words "absentee fathers." From the White

House to the house in your neighborhood, there are many voices and influencers, "instructors" as Paul said, but few real fathers. Because of this severe lack of the impartation of life, so many in both the culture and the church end up in the "jailhouse" or the "outhouse."

I refuse to stay at the level of growth that does not impart life to others. That would be so selfish and self-serving and void of love. Real love, the greatest love, is to give one's life (live one's life) for the benefit of others.[47] To impart life is to really know the One who is from the beginning—the originator—the source—the Creator—and to receive, retain, and reproduce his life in oneself, while also imparting it to others in his name.

In this manner of impartation, the desired destination that God has preplanned for his children becomes reachable. I have walked on this journey for many years and will continue to until my time is done, always holding up this standard and promise from God's Word:

> Then the LORD your God will bring you to the land which your fathers possessed and you shall possess it. He will prosper you and multiply you more than your fathers.[48]

In this way of continuing increase, the grace that God has bestowed upon us is not in vain as others benefit from our walk of faith.[49] I trust that there is an impartation quickening in your life right now as you spend it reading these words. Let's go to work on something that will last long after we ourselves are gone. Paul encouraged the church in Corinth in this way:

> Therefore, my beloved brethren, be steadfast, immovable, always abounding in the work of the Lord, knowing that your labor is not in vain in the Lord.[50]

As we mature in Christ, we can and are making a difference. Just as Paul acknowledged to the church in Philippi, I too am not claiming to have already attained a perfected life.[51] However, I do identify with the fathering spirit which was maturing in him so that he could declare,

> I press toward the goal for the prize of the upward call of God in Christ Jesus. Therefore let us, as many as are mature, have this mind; and if in anything you think otherwise, God will reveal even this to you.[52]

I trust that God is speaking to you in a way that will motivate you to a greater experience in his Kingdom. On this journey, we are not trailblazers; we are path finders. Jesus Christ our Lord said, "Follow Me."[53] It's as if our Lord has paved a great highway for us. All the tolls have been paid in full beforehand. It is the "freeway" to the Father's house!

The fathering, life imparting spirit in Paul also is an encouragement to us to travel this path that leads to fullness of life. He wrote, "Brethren, join in following my example, and note those who so walk [there are others], as you have us for a pattern."[54]

This brings us to the final step of the journey—a perfect (teleios) man, in the measure of the stature of the fullness of Christ.[55] There can be much confusion about this stature. From the context of Ephesians 4:13, it is clearly a stature that we do not achieve or arrive at as individuals but as the corporate Body of Christ. Paul said,

> ...till we all come to the unity of the faith and of the knowledge of the Son of God, to a perfect man, to the measure of the stature of the fullness of Christ.[56]

Here, Paul indicated that we have not yet arrived at the unity of the faith. We could express this concept of unity, as we already have in previous chapters, as becoming one with the great "One" identified in The Shema.

Paul indicates that while we are on this part of the journey we should be "endeavoring to keep the unity of the Spirit in the bond of peace."[57] Oh, the unity of the Holy Spirit! I have said so little about him and his role in all of this that we are discovering.

Suffice at this point to say that without him, we can never make such a journey. He is the guarantee of our inheritance.[58] We are sealed with the Holy Spirit of promise.[59] I will simply remind you of the things that Jesus said about this third person of the "One":

- He is the Helper.[60]
- He abides with us and in us forever.[61]
- He is the Spirit of truth.[62]
- He will teach us.[63]
- He will remind us of the words of Jesus.[64]
- He will testify of Jesus.[65]
- He will convict the world of sin, righteousness, and judgment.[66]

- He will guide us into all truth.[67]
- Whatever he hears he will speak.[68]
- He will tell us things to come.[69]
- He will glorify Jesus.[70]
- He will take what belongs to Jesus and declare it to us.[71]

Without him, we will never arrive at the "teleios" destination. Thank God not only for his Word but also for his Spirit!

There is much to be taught concerning "teleology," which is "the study of final causes, the definite end, the ultimate purpose for everything."[72] Selah. Selah. Selah. Pause—think about it. Meditate on it.

The prefix "tele" is a very important part of our English language. It is a transliteration of the Greek word "teleios." Our language is filled with so many words that begin with this prefix. As you read through the following list go slowly and think of what each word means and how important it is to our daily lives. Some of these words you will recognize right away and others you may have to—and it would be good for you to—look up in a dictionary.

- Telecast
- Telecommunication
- Telecommuting
- Teleconference
- Telecourse
- Telegony
- Telegram
- Telegraph

- Telekinesis
- Telemarketing
- Telemeter
- Teleology
- Teleonomy
- Telepathy
- Telephone
- Telephotography
- Teleportation
- Teleprocessing
- Telescope
- Telesis
- Telesthesia
- Teletext
- Telethon
- Teletype
- Television
- Telex

And last but not least, "televangelist." Uh oh, what have we here? I will drop this one like a hot potato!

The subject of "teleology" is too great to attempt to explain at this point in this book, but please don't hold that against me. I encourage you to search it out. Teleology is about where we are all supposed to be going—the final destination. I have written about it extensively in another book, "Truth Be Told," which is a sequel to "To the Unknown God." These books are available to you if you desire to read them. You can locate them in the same way that this book came into your hands. But what is most important is that as you are reading you have been locating yourself on the journey.

Suffice for now to say that "teleology" can be considered to be the study of "ripened fruit." This speaks of the great end-time harvest. Need I say more? That is a mouthful! Let's get on with the journey, step by step.

> Therefore be patient, brethren, until the coming of the Lord. See how the farmer waits for the precious fruit of the earth, waiting patiently for it until it receives the early and latter rain. You also be patient. Establish your hearts, for the coming of the Lord is at hand.
>
> James 5:7–8

THE JOURNEY
MAIN POINTS:

- As God's children we are to grow into "perfection."
- "Perfection" is the state of maturity.
- Growing up to maturity is a process, a journey.
- We should embrace the threefold concept of this journey as:
  - out of
  - into
  - on in or on to
- The stages of this journey are distinctly identified in the Greek translation of the New Testament as:
  - Teknon: a born one, infant.
  - Nepios: a toddler with "no words."
  - Paidion: a child under discipline and training.
  - Neaniskos: a youthful regenerated new man.
  - Huios: a full grown son (or daughter).
  - Pater: an imparter of life, a parent.
  - Teleios: a perfect, mature, full grown, complete adult.
- Without the help of the Holy Spirit we cannot complete this journey.

- The end of our journey can be likened to "ripened fruit" which speaks of the great end time harvest.

THE FAMILY

And I also say to you ... on this rock I will build My church, and the gates of Hades shall not prevail against it.

Matthew 16:18

When He had stopped speaking, He said to Simon, "Launch out into the deep and let down your nets for a catch."

Luke 5:4

God is the master mathematician. No matter how angels or men attempt to divide, subtract, or fractionalize his Word, it always sums up to the same total. Because he is "The Father," the summation of all things accomplished by the incarnation of truth will always add up to be "the family of God."

Although the word "family" is only used once in the New Testament, I believe that it really sums up what everything concerning the incarnation points to. It is the Greek word "patria" which means "paternal descent."[1] As we have seen, the word "pater" describes one who imparts life.[2]

The Scripture declares that "the Father has life in Himself...."[3] Therefore, all other life has descended down from he who dwells in the heaven of heavens.[4] This "paternal descent" includes everything that lives.

However, among all the creatures of God, man is specifically identified as being the only one created in his own image and likeness.[5] Being created in the image and likeness of God the Father, mature believers can be called "patriarchs," meaning "progenitors" or people of "first descent."[6] This means first in rank, chief, or principal among all of God's creatures.

Thereby the phrase "family of God," though generally used to include all that lives, specifically identifies mankind as a distinct genus or species of the "God kind." To be even more specific, it really describes the people of God in the new creation that has been made possible through the work of the threefold manifestation of Christ in the world.[7]

These are the people that Jesus referred to when he declared, "I will build My church."![8] The church is the family of God. This church is made up of a corporate assembly of redeemed men, women, and children who are "called out of" (the Greek word "ekklesia"[9]) darkness and "into" his marvelous light.[10] The church is a specifically "chosen generation" or "genus," a royal priesthood, a holy nation, God's own special people.[11]

The family of God is destined not only to be a people of "first descent" but also a people of "final ascent." The church is the first and final produce of the harvest of the precious fruit of the earth determined by God the Father as he sowed the life of his first fruit Son into the earth.

To coin a phrase, one could say that the church is the "teleological" family of the God-kind. Not only are we the product of the great gift of God's Son, we are also destined to be laborers in the great "end-time (teleology)" harvest that the husbandman is waiting patiently for.[12]

The compassion of our Lord Jesus for this great harvest of the souls of men—who were weary and scattered, like sheep having no shepherd—caused him to declare unto his disciples, "The harvest truly is plentiful, but the laborers are few. Therefore pray the Lord of the harvest to send out laborers into his harvest."[13]

Through the examples of the gospels, we know that Jesus likened working in the harvest field to "fishing for men."[14] The disciples learned many great lessons about the harvest from their life experiences of casting their nets into the sea. In fact, one of the parables of Jesus concerning the end of the age (teleology) is about the kingdom of heaven being like a dragnet that is cast into the sea, gathering fish (men) of every kind.[15]

The dragnet of God is a very important concept. When I look at a globe or a map of the world, I can't help but see the crossing lines of longitude and latitude that cover the whole earth. It's a net!

Of course, these lines are imaginary but nevertheless they speak prophetically of how the kingdom of heaven and the knowledge of the glory of God cover the earth just as the waters cover the sea.[16] God certainly has the harvest of the whole world in mind![17]

Referring to the opening Scripture from Luke 5, I would like you to "launch out into the deep" with me to see if we can be as "astonished" as the disciples of Jesus were at so great a catch of fish.[18]

To briefly rehearse the account, Luke recorded that Jesus had sat down in a local fisherman's boat to teach the multitude about the kingdom of God. Because the people were on the shoreline, the boat was only put out a little from the land in shallow water.[19]

Shallow water is usually a safe place to be. However, there are not many fish (souls of men) to be harvested in shallow water. Too many of our brothers and sisters in Christ live much of their lives in such a shallow place. In the gospel story, Jesus was teaching a multitude but really "fishing" for the fishermen whom he would soon call to be his disciples.[20]

In order to really "catch" them, Jesus stopped speaking to the others and told Simon (Peter) to "launch out into the deep…for a catch."[21] Of course, Simon was not only about to haul in a great catch but along with a few others be caught (harvested) himself.

As you launch out into the deep with me, I'll be right up front and honest with you, I am hoping to "catch" you with the incarnation of truth that has "caught" me! Let's venture out into the deep together.

As the story is recorded in the gospels, the fishermen complained that they had toiled at fishing all night and caught nothing.[22] Unfortunately, this is the current condition of many of the members of the family of God, who are toiling in boats called local churches or who are standing alone on piers casting a line instead of a net.

However, in Luke's account, when the disciples heeded the word of the Lord, they indeed caught a great number of fish. Then something very important happened that taught the disciples a lesson that much of today's church still hasn't learned. Their net was broken![23] The catch, the harvest, was in danger of being lost.

What did the disciples do? They signaled to their partners in another boat to come and help them. As the others came, they indeed helped, but the catch was so great that both boats began to sink![24] Here again, this is the current condition of so many members of the family of God. Boats are sinking everywhere, from the home to the church, to the school, to the city, to the nation!

What has all this to do with the incarnation of truth and the family of God? If you can venture out into the deep with me, we can apprehend an important "catch." Having the church of our Lord Jesus Christ built on the rock and fishing for the souls of men with nets that do not break and boats that do not sink can be considered synonymous (or at the very least similar). As we "catch" on to this concept, we can say that we've just moved from shallow water into deep water.

I believe that we must have nets that do not break and boats that do not sink. As the pastor of a local church for almost twenty-eight years, I can tell you that our net has broken more than once and that our boat has almost sunk at least twice!

This is happening all around us and few are finding the solution. I believe the words of our Lord when he declared, "I will build My church and the gates of Hades shall not prevail against [break or sink] it."[25]

Some many years ago, without even a personal meeting or salutation, a man of God with the word of the Lord in his mouth preached at a convention of our family of local churches and saved our boat from sinking.[26] He imagined Jesus declaring the truth about building his church to sound like this:

> **I** will build my church!
> I **WILL** build my church!
> I will **BUILD** my church!
> I will build **MY** church!
> I will build My **CHURCH**!
> I WILL BUILD MY CHURCH!

I got it! Do you get it? Try these words in your mouth and see how they taste! Hearing yourself declare the words of Jesus may just pop your ears open like when you are gaining altitude in a jumbo jet. This is all about the word of God and the faith that it brings when it is heard.[27]

The Scripture declares in the book of Job that "the ear tests words as the palate tastes food."[28] I am going to present words to you concerning the "rock" that Jesus is building his church on and the family of God. I believe that as you read my words—which are based upon God's Word—that faith will arise in you and we can help one another mend our broken nets and strengthen our threatened boats. Test and taste these words, but be ready for a hearty meal of something strong and revolutionary.

First of all, we must all stop trying to build Christ's church. Let's learn how to be his church. There are certain "models" for the church revealed in the biblical blueprints and looking at them will be very helpful for us to see how we, the church, look to God.

Let me help you understand what I mean by a model. If a man walked into your presence in a brightly colored uniform with a number on the back and was wearing a hat with a single bill at its front and was carrying a bat in one hand and a glove in the other, what "model" would you think he was portraying? I think you would say, "Baseball." Isn't that right?

Now, if another man walked up to you dressed in a similar manner but was wearing a helmet with a huge face mask on his head, and big pads on his shoulders and thighs, and was carrying an odd shaped ball in his hands, what "model" would you think he was portraying? Football! Isn't that right? The world is filled with models.

What are the New Testament models for the church that Jesus is building? A simple look at the writings of the apostle Paul and other apostles will reveal that they identified at least five different models for the church:

- A body
- A bride
- A temple
- An army
- A family

Let's take a brief look at each model and see what we can learn from them. First we have the body, specifically the body of Christ. Paul wrote, "Now you are the body of Christ, and members individually."[29] He declared that God has set every member of the body into the body, just as it pleased him to do, just as the hands and feet and other essential members of our own bodies are set.[30]

Another model for the New Testament church that Paul identified is a bride, specifically the bride of Christ. When giving instruction concerning the marital relationship of a husband and wife, Paul clearly stated that all of his teaching about this relationship was really about the relationship between Christ and the church.[31] In this relationship, Christ is to be considered to be the husband and the church the wife.[32]

The apostle John also gave us insight into the model of the bride. In the book of Revelation, he recorded the words of a great angel that declared the church to be "the bride, the Lamb's wife."[33] John also recorded a thunderous announcement that the marriage supper of the Lamb (Jesus) and his wife (the church) had come to the time of commencement.[34]

A body and a bride are both biblical models for the church. Another vivid scriptural model found in the New Testament for the church is that of a temple. Both of the apostles Peter and Paul described the church in such a way. Peter called the church an edifice of "living stones" built up as a spiritual house (a temple).[35] Paul wrote that the whole household of God, the church, was being built together into a holy temple in the Lord to be a habitation of God in the Spirit.[36]

We also find in the apostle Paul's writing that he described the church in the context of an army. He instructed the saints at Ephesus to be clothed in the whole armor of God. Equipped in such a military manner, the saints were to wrestle, or cast off, principalities, powers, rulers of the darkness of this age and spiritual hosts (armies) of wickedness in the heavenly places.[37]

Since Paul had written this epistle to the saints in Ephesus and not to a specific individual as he did at other times, it is appropriate to understand his words to be addressing not only an armed man but an army of men. It is therefore appropriate to consider an army, specifically the Army of God, to be another valid model for the church.

Finally, we can find in the New Testament at least one more beautiful and vivid model for the church. The church is not only described as a body, a bride, a temple, and an army but also as a family—specifically the family of God.

In the context of the fellowship of the mystery of the incarnation of Christ in the world, the apostle Paul declared something awesome concerning the eternal purpose of God that was accomplished in Christ Jesus our Lord. He declared that God was going to make "all people see" the fellowship of this mystery and that the "manifold wisdom" of God would be made known by the church to the entire invisible spiritual world in the heavenly places.[38]

Paul apprehended the great mystery of the dispensation of the grace of God that was to grant, even to the Gentiles, opportunity to enter into fellowship with God. In appreciation of such an extravagant manifestation of love Paul wrote, "For this reason I bow my knees to the Father of our Lord Jesus Christ, from whom the whole family in heaven and earth is named."[39]

Yes, another beautiful and scripturally accurate model for the New Testament church is the family of God! This is the great "catch" that has "caught" me as I have launched out into the deep. Please, do not head back to shore just yet. We can go much deeper!

For further understanding about the church that Jesus is building, according to the eternal purpose accomplished by the incarnation of truth, let us briefly look at each of these models and see what type of leadership model goes with each of them. We will find that much can be learned from each example. We can discover what model may be best in order to see nets built that do not break and boats built that do not sink.

What is the leadership paradigm for the body? It is the head, isn't that right? Jesus Christ our Lord is the head of the body. What about the bride? As head of the body, Jesus Christ is also the husband of the bride.[40] These two paradigms really go together. The leadership paradigms are headship for the body and husbandman for the bride.

What about the temple? What is the leadership paradigm for the temple? Jesus Christ our Lord is recognized as being the cornerstone of the temple. Concerning the temple of "living stones," the apostle Peter wrote of Jesus as being the "chief cornerstone," elect and precious.[41] Of course, it is the cornerstone of any building that is the benchmark to insure that it is constructed properly and upright.

What about the army? What is the leadership paradigm for an army? It is officers, isn't that right? In the natural, we have generals, colonels, majors, captains, and lieutenants as officers to lead an army. In the New Testament Scripture, we find Jesus is referred to as the "captain" of our salvation.[42] Please don't regard the spiritual office of "captain" as being lower than a natural army's general or other officers but as the highest rank in the host (army) of the Lord.[43]

In the New Testament, we also see that Jesus, as highest ranking officer of the Army of God, has also delegated "official" authority to others under him who are to use those offices to equip the saints for the work of the ministry (which includes warfare).[44] Of course, I am speaking of those Jesus commissions as apostles, prophets, evangelists, pastors, and teachers.[45] Because of the way men have so magnified these offices and officers, I feel it necessary to point out that all of what we call the "fivefold" ministry offices are only temporary.

Yes, it is true. They are all temporary. It is written that all of these officers are duly commissioned to lead the church until "we all come to the unity of the faith and of the knowledge of the Son of God, to a perfect [teleios] man, to the measure of the stature of the fullness of Christ."[46]

Notice the ultimate purpose for such a military leadership paradigm. It's so that the saints, the members of the body, the bride of Christ, the living stones of the temple, and the soldiers of the army of God can come to the knowledge—not of the head of the body, not of the husband of the bride, not of the cornerstone of the temple, or of the captain of the army—but to the knowledge of the Son of God! This is really all about family—specifically, the family of God!

Before we address the leadership paradigm for the family and its major significance to nets that do not break and boats that do not sink, please allow me a very important sidebar. Like the apostle Paul, I am very jealous for the church with a godly jealousy.[47]

All of the models we have referred to for the church are biblical and valid. However, many of the brethren in our nation are using a very different model to pattern the church after. It is the corporate business model. I do not believe it is scripturally valid for the church to be in business, in the way that those in the secular world are.

We must recognize that as citizens of the United States of America we are living in a business culture based upon free enterprise capitalism. This culture tends to dominate all subcultures existing under its strong influence.

Please do not misunderstand. I am not against capitalism or making a profit. We learn from the Scripture that the Lord gives his people the power to get wealth, but we must know why. It is written, "And you shall remember the LORD your God, for it is He who gives you power to get wealth, that He may establish His covenant...."[48]

Before I say more, please let me assure you, the reader, of my patriotism. I am a natural-born citizen of the United States and served our country as a platoon sergeant in an infantry company during the Vietnam war. I pledge my allegiance to the United States of America, but first and foremost I pledge my loyalty to the highest royalty—the Lord Jesus Christ!

There is a spirit of greed running through our nation and the church often fails to overcome it. Essentially, the essence of biblical economics is found in much deeper water than in the system of capitalism. Ideally, in the kingdom of God, money is not really designed for buying and selling but for giving and receiving. Greed is not a biblical motivation. Greed is selfish, self-serving, and destructive.

There is no biblical model for the church to emulate a greedy form of capitalism. The kind of economic pursuit that so many in our church culture are succumbing to is also in direct violation of the creation principle of the Sabbath.[49] In our fast moving, high-octane, financial "pressure cooker" lifestyle, who among us ever takes a real rest? I'm not talking about a vacation or a three-day weekend. I'm speaking of a biblical Sabbath where no "customary work" is done.[50] How many church leaders promote a real Sabbath for their congregations?

When local churches and denominations adopt a business model for their blueprints, they are usually in danger of ending up with broken nets and sinking boats. Violation of the Sabbath was considered a capital crime in the Old Testament and was punishable by death.[51] This issue is that serious.

Nets that are never washed or mended properly are usually damaged beyond repair. Boats that never have their leaks repaired will surely eventually sink. Such is the case with so many of the churches around our nation. They have adopted a business model for their paradigm and we are all suffering as a result.

Always "doing business" is not a legitimate model for the church. By the way, what is the leadership paradigm for a business model? It is CEOs, CFOs, and a board of corporate officers. There are far too many gospel ships sailing the waters of our nation today being led by CEO and CFO types. They may grow big and take on a lot of passengers, but I do not think they will be able to hold their own cargo or reach their destination. Look around. Let's get back to the biblical blueprints!

Getting back to the biblical models for the church of our Lord Jesus Christ, we find that we paused at the model of the family. Let's continue. What is the leadership paradigm for the family? It is father and mother—parents.

Just what is the "rock" on which the Lord is building his church on? While I believe that all of the models we have examined are biblically valid (except the business model), I do believe that the word of God clearly establishes one above all others that will insure the gates of Hades will not overcome it. It is the best one for acquiring nets that do not break and boats that do not sink.

It is the family model. Let me explain. Please keep in mind what I've already stated. Our teleios destination is to come to the knowledge of the Son of God. It is through Christ's Sonship that we can get to know him as head of the body, husband of the bride, cornerstone of the temple, and captain of the army. This will become clear as we look at the context of the statement of Jesus when he said, "I will build My church...."[52]

In a discourse with his disciples (fishers of men), Jesus asked them about who others were saying he was.[53] After numerous responses, Jesus continued to "catch" his disciples. He asked them, "But who do you say that I am?"[54]

It was Peter and only Peter who answered and said, "You are the Christ, the Son of the living God."[55] Jesus immediately recognized the source of such a powerful revelation given to a mere man of flesh and blood. No one could have revealed the identity of the incarnation of the person of truth in such an accurate way except the One from whom he came. It was the Father in heaven who gave Peter this astounding revelation that Jesus was the Son of God.[56]

At this point Jesus, blessed Peter and declared that this was the rock upon which he would build his church. Some would say that Peter was the rock, but this cannot be substantiated. In the Greek language, the "rock" is "petra" and means "a mass of rock."[57] "Petros," which was the name given to Peter by Jesus, means "a piece of rock."[58] It was as if Jesus was blessing Peter and affectionately telling him, "You are a chip off the old block. You are right. You are all right. I am the Christ, the Son of God!"

The "rock" is the revelation given to Peter by the Father, not Peter himself. The Father did not identify Jesus as the head of the body, the husband of the bride, the cornerstone of the temple, or the captain of the army but as the Son of the Father, the Son of God!

Please recognize that Jesus is known by many titles in many ways. Throughout Scripture, he is called:

- Prophet[59]
- Priest[60]
- King (of Kings)[61]
- Lord (of Lords)[62]
- Alpha and Omega[63]
- Beginning and End[64]
- Author and finisher of our faith[65]
- Lamb of God[66]
- Bright and Morning Star[67]
- Son of Man[68]
- Word of God[69]
- Faithful and True[70]
- Wonderful[71]
- Counselor[72]
- Mighty God[73]
- Everlasting Father[74]
- Prince of Peace[75]
- Lion of Judah[76]
- Root of David[77]
- The Branch[78]

Yes indeed, all of these names and titles are a revelation of who Jesus is. But you will notice the Father does not directly refer to Jesus using any of these accurate and biblical names.

The Father revealed the identity of Jesus to Peter as being the Christ, the Son of the living God. This revelation came somehow by the Spirit to Peter's inner man. There is no mention of Peter hearing God's audible voice at this time and in this place. However, there are accounts in the gospels where the Father's reference to Jesus was audibly spoken and heard.

As recorded in the New Testament, the first time that God the Father's voice is literally heard in the incarnate life of the Word of God is found just prior to the beginning of the ministry of Jesus. The young man Jesus of Nazareth, coming to a "fullness of time," made his way down to the river Jordan to be baptized by John the Baptist.[79]

John the Baptist was a unique and significant forerunner of the ministry of Jesus. He was "the voice of one crying in the wilderness: 'Prepare the way of the LORD; Make His paths straight.'"[80] John had a very specific ministry and was operating in the spirit and power of Elijah, an Old Testament prophet.[81] Please keep this ministry in mind. At the close of this chapter, you will clearly see its significance as part of the great "ripened fruit" end-time harvest.

The ministry of John the Baptist in preparing the way of the Lord was primarily an expression of a "fathering" spirit from the heart of Father God. His specific anointing would "turn the hearts of fathers to the children"[82] and "turn the hearts of the children to their fathers."[83]

Jesus declared concerning himself that Elijah must come before him and restore (or appoint[84]) all things.[85] Jesus had a specific appointment in time and space in order to begin his earthly ministry. Jesus could not begin his earthly ministry without first submitting himself to this "spirit and power of Elijah" that John the Baptist was anointed with. John realizing that Jesus was "the Lamb of God who takes away the sin of the world"[86] and that Jesus was greater than himself, hesitated at baptizing him and tried to prevent it.[87]

Jesus, however, knew that he must first submit to this "fathering spirit" before he could be declared to be who he really was. He communicated to John that it must be this way to fulfill all righteousness.[88]

Immediately, as Jesus came up from the waters of John's baptism, something absolutely wonderful and unprecedented happened. The heavens were opened and the Spirit of God descended from the Father (remember "patria" which means "paternal descent" or "family") like a dove and lit upon him.[89]

Suddenly, a voice came from heaven (from the same source as Peter's revelation concerning Christ's identity) and openly declared, "This is My beloved Son, in whom I am well pleased."[90] There it is again! Can you hear it? Can you see it? This is clearly the "rock." This is the "rock" of revelation—that Jesus the Christ is the Son of God. He is the One who is to restore the family of God! This is the "rock" upon which Jesus is building his church.

The Father did not declare Jesus to be his Prophet, Priest, King or any of the other significant names and titles that truly belong to him. The Father declared him to be his own Son! "Father" and "Son" are family words; the family of God is the summation of the threefold work of the incarnation!

Such an event is recorded to have happened again in the life and ministry of Jesus. Soon after, Peter received the heavenly revelation of the true identity of Jesus, the same revelation was also given to James and

John. Along with Jesus and Peter, they all went up to a mountaintop to pray. As Jesus prayed, he was transfigured before them. His face shone like the sun and his clothing became white as light.[91] He was speaking with the Old Testament prophets, Moses and Elijah "of His decease which He was about to accomplish in Jerusalem."[92]

Suddenly, a bright cloud overshadowed them and a voice came out of the cloud saying, "This is My beloved Son, in whom I am well pleased. Hear him!'"[93] Hear him? Can we "hear him" today?

And what would be the summation of all of the words of the one revealed to be the "Son" of God? Would it not be:

> I and my Father are one. No one comes to the Father except through Me. In my Father's house are many mansions; if it were not so, I would have told you. I go to prepare a place for you. And he who loves me will be loved by My Father, and I will love him and manifest Myself to him…and My Father will love him, and We will come to him and make Our home with him.[94]

Our home, our father, our family! In light of all these things, it is obvious to me that the family is the main ministry model of Jesus. Of course, Jesus fulfills all of the other biblical models for ministry as well because he himself is the fullness of every biblical model. However, his highest identity is as the Son of God.

Jesus always prayed to the Father and he taught us to pray to the Father. He taught us to begin our prayer by saying "our Father."[95] That simple phrase ministers to us above and beyond all other ministry models.

"Our Father" means that we are in the same "patria"—family of paternal descent; the same "genus"—species of the God-kind as Jesus Christ himself is! That net will "catch" and hold many souls of men and nothing will ever sink that boat!

No gate of Hades will ever prevail against such a rock. Through the threefold purpose accomplished by the incarnation of truth:

- Our sins have been taken away for his name's sake.
- The works of the devil have been destroyed.
- Having become one with God, we are now the "family of God."

This is what everything all around us is all about. The whole creation is waiting for the manifestation of God's family.[96] To make this a reality, Jesus came to show us not something but someone. Who did he come to show us? He came to show us the Father.[97] Jesus said, "I am the way, the truth, and the life. No one comes to the Father except through Me."[98]

I see something here. If we will cooperate with what Jesus is building, upon the rock he is building it on, we'll have nets that don't break. They will cover the world. We'll have boats that won't sink.

However, I see a major problem in our culture, in our generation. We are not cooperating with God's priorities. I believe that the leadership model God wants to build a church with and to establish in the church is the family. That is the original model of the manifestation of the image of God in the world.

God made a man and was very happy with the man until he looked at him and said it's not good for the man to be alone.[99] At creation, the man already had the woman inside of him. So God put a sleep on the man, and with what he took out of the man God made a helper comparable to him—a woman—and thus created a family.[100]

We should be teaching this model to our children. In our boat, we teach our young men that if they want a bride, a wife, a mate for life then they must go to sleep like the first man did. Father God will put such a beautiful sleep on any son who will surrender to it. We also tell them to keep their eyes closed, but dreaming is okay!

We teach our young women in the same manner. We teach them that using what comes from the side of a sleeping son, Father God will fashion them into a true daughter of the kingdom and at the appropriate time present them to the man of their dreams.

That is the original model, my friend. The family of God! Jesus himself fulfilled this pattern and slept the sleep of death that through the piercing of his own side a woman could come forth who would be bone of his bones and flesh of his flesh.[101] As the crucified Son of God, Jesus qualified to receive his helper, the church, and start a "new creation" family. What a magnificent story! It is colossal compared to all others.

It is a tragedy that we see so little of this today in our modern church culture. Instead, we find men and women of God that are so powerfully anointed but who are working with the wrong model, and as a result their own homes are falling apart. They do not have a holy, undefiled, matrimonial bed at home and do not raise their children biblically, and then they become prey for evil. They are living out their faith based upon the wrong model. Their nets are breaking and their ships are sinking. There is no denying it.

We may not be able to deny it, but we sure can fix it. We are called to come out from a cultural, nominal Christianity into experiencing the power of the three-fold revelation of the incarnation of truth. I assure you that I not only speak and write these things but as a husband, father, and member of a local church family I also live them.

What on earth is the church, the family of God, here for if not to fulfill the God-given ministry of rec-onciliation? It's as if God were pleading through us, imploring others on Christ's behalf, to be reconciled to the heavenly Father.[102]

What does such a ministry really look like? How does it work? Is it a hospital to mend a broken body? Is it a prenuptial counseling session between soon-to-be spouses?

Is it a construction project to erect an edifice? Is it a "boot camp" to train up an army?

Yes. The answer, as we have seen, is yes to all of the above. However, greater than all of that, the true min-istry of reconciliation is biblically likened to the way mothers and fathers raise and love their children. Based on all that I have shared, I trust that you are beginning to see that the predominant model for the church is the family.

A brief look at one of the most effective apostolic and prophetic team ministries that we know about will bear witness to this truth. I am referring to the apostle Paul and his prophetic ministry team.[103] I would like to exegete Paul's own description of this ministry from his first epistle to the church in Thessalonica. Remember that the ear tests words like the palate tastes food. As you test and taste the words that follow, I can't help but believe that you will taste and see that the Lord is good.[104]

In some cases, our English translation of the Scriptures does not fully express the meaning of the Greek language; therefore, it is necessary to refer back to the Greek words, as we have been doing. One of the clearest examples of the need to study in this way is found in what we will read now.

In his epistle to the church in Thessalonica, Paul described the ministry of his team as being approved and entrusted by God to deliver the ministry in such a way as to please God and not according to the expectations of men.[105] Paul did not magnify his office, however, he did acknowledge that as approved apostles of God his team could have made demands on the church as they ministered to them but did not do so.[106]

Rather, quite the opposite occurred. This man of great power and his seasoned ministry team behaved in a manner worthy of the Lord and of the Father in heaven. Here is the description of the ministry of reconciliation in Paul's own words:

> But we were gentle among you, just as a nursing
> mother cherishes her own children. So, affec-
> tionately longing for you, we were well pleased
> to impart to you not only the gospel of God,
> but also our own lives, because you had become
> dear to us.[107]

Now, this translation needs no help! What a word
picture. One might not have expected it as a description of so strong a man as Paul and his powerful ministry team. Nevertheless, the way Paul describes the
ministry bears repeating:

- Gentle
- Nursing mother
- Cherishing
- Affectionately longing
- Imparting
- Spending one's own life
- Endearing

I think it amazing that such a powerful minister of
the gospel as Paul could describe his service as being
like a gently nursing mother's ministry. This is the
man who could cast out devils and strike enemies with
blindness![108] He was so powerful that even handker-
chiefs taken from his body could heal the sick![109]

This is the man who wrote much of our New
Testament Bible. So much of what we know of God
comes from what Paul called "my gospel."[110] Many of
the brethren do not even know that Paul preached his
own gospel apart from the gospels written by Matthew,
Mark, Luke, and John.

Paul's gospel is primarily about the ongoing ministry of the Son of God after his resurrection and ascension. It is really about the ongoing present-day ministry of Jesus Christ through his church, and Paul describes it as the ministry of a gentle, nursing mother—a family model and paradigm!

As Paul continued to describe his and his team's ministry, he changes his wording but not his model. This is where we need the help of a Greek dictionary. Paul wrote, "…as you know how we exhorted, and comforted, and charged every one of you, as a father does his own children."[111]

Now, we easily recognize that fatherly exhortation is a good thing. The comfort of a father is a good thing also. A father's charge to his children is certainly a good thing. However, the truth of what Paul wrote is much, much better than good.

The original Greek word used by Paul and translated as "exhorted" is "parakaleo." This is a powerful compound word that means "call near to oneself."[112] This word picture describes the true heart of a father—closeness and intimacy.

This is definitely not a word picture of someone in authority who just runs things from afar—usually from a place above and beyond everyone else. This is the description of someone who can be seen and touched and known intimately. It does not necessarily speak of a "famous" person but rather speaks of one who is intimately "well known." This is a far better model for ministry.

This is the way of a true father. Paul expands the word picture with the Greek word "paramutheomai" which is translated as "comforted."[113] The true meaning of this once again powerful compound word is "to draw near and tell a story to." The root of the word is the English word "myth" which means "a story." As in the previous compound word, the prefix "para" means "near" or "close to."[114]

These words are describing true biblical, effective fatherly ministry. The words draw a picture of a daddy calling to his son or daughter to come and sit on his lap so that he can relate a story to them from firsthand knowledge and experience.

Of course, in the context of Paul's writing, the story is about Jesus, the Son of God and about the Father's great love. This is the gospel! This is the good news that should be preached and presented to everyone in a way such as this.

This kind of biblical father will tell his children about Adam, Noah, Abraham, Joseph, Moses, David, Peter, James, John, Paul, and all the others—all in the context of Jesus the Son of God and the heavenly Father.

Most important of all, a true biblical father will tell his children what God has done in his life and the life of his family and how they are following the Lord. He also tells them about what great things God will do in their own lives as they receive the revelation of truth.

This is the model of ministry that really works. This is what comforts and exhorts a natural or spiritual child to know the living God and to live for him. This is what makes a net that won't break and a boat that won't sink.

It's the time-tested family model as revealed in the word of God: "The living, the living man, he shall praise You, as I do this day; the father shall make known Your truth to the children."[115]

This is good. It gets even better, much better. Paul completed his description of this family ministry model by using the word that was translated "charged." This is the Greek word "martureo," which is more accurately transliterated "martyr."[116] A martyr is a witness. A witness testifies of truth in a judicial setting. A judgment will be made based on the testimony of a witness. Someone will make a decision based upon what they hear and see.

Be mindful that a true minister of the gospel is neither a judge nor a jury member. Neither is he a prosecuting or defense attorney. He certainly is not the defendant, although he was once on trial himself.

A real biblical father is a martyr, a witness to the truth. His own life produces the evidence that the "up close and personal" stories he tells are true. He provides indisputable evidence that the stories he tells of God are the real thing. He never magnifies nor exalts himself (though as Paul said, as an apostle he could have).

According to this family model, a father calls his child (natural and/or spiritual) to himself and points him to God, assuring him that he too can have this kind of intimate relationship with the heavenly Father.

Let me paraphrase in my own words just what Paul was saying to the church:

> As you know we called you near to sit beside us,
> or on our lap like a father with his children. We

told you all that we have learned about the good news of the gospel of the kingdom of God and how it has worked in us and through us. The fruit of our own lives is a continuing witness to you that our words are true! You can count on it![117]

This is it! This is what is missing in today's church world. The family model provides a true living epistle of Father God's love. There is no refuting it because it is the incarnation of truth in a human vessel like me or you. Paul knew it. He wrote, "I have been crucified with Christ; it is no longer I who live, but Christ lives in me...."[118]

Here is how and why it works. Paul continued his description by saying,

> For this reason we also thank God without ceasing, because when you received the word of God which you heard from us, you welcomed it not as the word of men, but as it is in truth, the word of God, which also effectively works in you who believe.[119]

What more can we want? Read that verse again! Using the family model of the "rock" on which Christ is building his church, we gently nurse, we cherish, we show affection, we impart life, and we spend our own life for those endeared to us. We also call them near, tell them about God's love, and produce the proof of what we are saying to them. And then they receive the truth and it works in them. The word continues its incarnation! This is wonderful! No other model of the church works quite like this one does!

This is the model that will change the world. As I have stated, I wholeheartedly believe that the family model is the "rock" upon which Jesus is building his church. It is the revelation of the family of God. This is the model for the twenty-first century church to return to.

It has been said that the church builds strong families. That is not quite true. It is better said that God uses strong families to build the church. Don't wait on your local church to adopt this model. Start it right at home in your own life.

As you make this adjustment in your life, you and yours (whether few or many) will become stronger members of the greater family of the church in the world. This is the essence of what Jesus said when he declared,

> If two of you agree on earth concerning any-
> thing that they ask, it will be done for them by
> My Father in heaven. For where two or three
> are gathered together in My name, I am there
> in the midst of them.[120]

Too many leaders in today's church world ignore the admonition of Paul to Timothy, his son in the faith, concerning bishops. Bishops are simply church overseers. Paul insisted that the prerequisite for the ministry of a bishop was that they were to first rule their own house well and then minister in the house of God.[121]

First at home, then in the church; why have we forsaken such a simple, pure model?

I would like to close this chapter with something prophetic and wonderful concerning God's plan for today's church as it relates to the great "ripened fruit" end-time "teleios" harvest.

Is it possible that something as simple as being a good dad, a good mom or child, could "catch" the people of the world in a net that doesn't break and establish them on the "rock" in a boat that won't sink? Is that too simple a thing?

I certainly greatly appreciate all the models for the church found in the New Testament. However, I must tell you that it won't be "heads" of great ministries that change the world. It won't be the ecclesiastic leaders who incorrectly consider themselves to be "husbands" married to God's bride who will change the world. Neither will it be the "cornerstone" layers of God's holy temple, nor the great "generals" of his awesome army that change the world.

Who will it be then? It will be those that are making all people see the mystery of the fellowship of Christ and making the manifold wisdom of God known to the creatures inhabiting the invisible realm.[122] It will be the dads, moms, sons, and daughters of the family of God!

How can I say this? This is exactly what has been prophesied. Do you recall how I asked you to remember the "spirit and power of Elijah" as manifested in the life of John the Baptist, the forerunner of Christ?

This is the ministry that prepares the way and makes ready a people for the coming of the Lord.[123] As it was then at the first coming of Christ, so it will also be at his return. Without this ministry, the harvest will not happen.

The ministers of Christ should not just "catch" the souls of men in their net, taking them "out of" without bringing them "on in" and "into" something that will not break or sink. What is God's plan then? It is written, "A father of the fatherless, a defender of widows, is God in His holy habitation. God sets the solitary in families...."[124]

The ministry of the "spirit and power of Elijah" is a family ministry. It is a trumpet ministry that precedes and announces the coming of the Lord. According to the Word of God, this trumpet ministry, this voice crying in the wilderness, accomplishes five mighty things.

In the Old Testament it is written,

> Behold, I will send you Elijah the prophet before the coming of the great and dreadful day of the LORD. And he will turn the hearts of the fathers to the children, and the hearts of the children to their fathers, lest I come and strike the earth with a curse.[125]

And again it is written in the New Testament,

> And he will turn many of the children of Israel to the Lord their God. He will also go before him in the spirit and power of Elijah, 'to turn the hearts of the fathers to the children,' and the disobedient to the wisdom of the just, to make ready a people prepared for the Lord.[126]

These Scriptures were historically fulfilled at the first coming of Christ, as John the Baptist recognized Him and announced His arrival to not only the nation of Israel but also the whole world. John declared, "Behold! The Lamb of God who takes away the sin of the world!"[127]

The Scriptures also have a further prophetic fulfillment. A great "Elijah Company" of the sons and daughters of God are, in our day and age, raising their voices as John the Baptist once did and declaring,

> The voice of one crying in the wilderness: Prepare the way of the Lord; make His paths straight. Every valley shall be filled and every mountain and hill brought low; the crooked places shall be made straight and the rough ways smooth; and all flesh shall see the salvation of God.[128]

Let's take a close look at the power released by this specific ministry. First, it turns the hearts of the fathers to the children. It is not the hearts of kings, presidents, senators, congressmen, CEOs, entrepreneurs, doctors, lawyers, or church officials that get turned. It's the hearts of fathers.

It's not that any of these people are not fathers, but their hearts are presently given over to the cares of this world, the deceitfulness of riches, the desire for other things, and the pleasures of life that choke the word of God and bring no fruit to maturity (end-time harvest).[129]

This first "turning" of the hearts of fathers is the beginning of a "revolution." A revolution is a rotation, a turning. It is a "returning" to a staring point—the original plan of God! It is an "overturning" of the rebellion that brought the curse. This turning of the hearts of the fathers brings a revival, a reformation, and the restoration of all things to the glory of God!

The second great thing accomplished by the power of this ministry is the turning of the hearts of the children to their fathers. This revolution will bring healing to homes and restore the sanctity and holiness of the family. The generations will be blessed according to the first commandment given by God that contains a promise: "Honor your father and mother...that it may be well with you and you may live long on the earth."[130]

As this restoration takes place, the blessing promised by God to families that live for him will be fulfilled. During the time of preparation to enter the Promised Land in the Old Testament, the Lord blessed the fathers and mothers who would diligently teach their children the ways of the Lord.[131]

These inspired words spoken to them by Moses are a blessing and a prophetic principle that can be understood in context of the great end-time harvest: "May the LORD God of your fathers make you a thousand times more numerous than you are, and bless you as He has promised you!"[132]

Concerning the children, the Lord also spoke a blessing through Moses that rings true to us today as a prophetic generation who are proclaiming the testimony of Jesus.[133] Moses declared,

> Then the LORD your God will bring you to the
> land which your fathers possessed, and you shall
> possess it. He will prosper you and multiply you
> more than your fathers.[134]

Through the spirit of such rich blessing, the necessity to strike the earth with a curse as God warned through the prophecy of Malachi is reversed! This is the third great work that this ministry accomplishes. Once again, the family of God can "be fruitful and multiply; fill the earth and subdue it; [and] have dominion" in it.[135]

And then the fourth great revolution is accomplished through such a wonderful ministry. It is the harvest of ripened fruit, the "teleology" of the plan of God. It is the essence of the true evangelistic spirit of the gospel of the kingdom of heaven. It is surely written that he will also "turn the disobedient [hearts] to the wisdom of the just...."[136] Think about that!

Just what is the wisdom of the just? It is a life based upon the completed threefold work accomplished by the incarnation of truth. It is right living. It is living as the righteousness of God in Christ.[137] The Proverbs speak clearly about the wisdom of the just:

> Wisdom calls aloud outside; she raises her
> voice in the open squares. She cries out in the
> chief concourses, at the openings of the gates
> in the city...Turn...surely I will pour out my
> spirit upon you...Happy is the man who finds
> wisdom...her proceeds are better than the prof-
> its of silver, and her gain than fine gold. She is
> more precious than rubies, and all the things you

may desire cannot compare with her. Length of days is in her right hand, in her left hand riches and honor. Her ways are ways of pleasantness, and all her paths are peace. She is a tree of life to those who take hold of her, and happy are all who retain her. The wise shall inherit glory. Does not wisdom cry out, and understanding lift up her voice? She takes her stand on the top of the high hill, beside the way, where the paths meet. She cries out by the gates, at the entry of the city, at the entrance of the doors: "To you, O men, I call, and my voice is to the sons of men. O you simple ones, understand prudence, and you fools be of an understanding heart. Listen, for I will speak of excellent things, and from the opening of my lips will come right things; for my mouth will speak truth…For whoever finds me finds life, and obtains favor from the Lord." Wisdom has built her house, she has hewn out her seven pillars; How much better to get wisdom than gold! Through wisdom a house is built…My son, eat honey because it is good, and the honeycomb which is sweet to your taste; so shall the knowledge of wisdom be to your soul; if you have found it, there is a prospect, and your hope will not be cut off. Whoever loves wisdom makes his father rejoice…[138]

Who would not desire such a life? When our heavenly Father rejoices over us, heaven has indeed come to earth! This is what will attract the disobedient and motivate them to turn to the wisdom of the just.

This is the message and the ministry that prepares the way of the Lord. The fifth great blessing that is accomplished is that a people are made ready for him! Our great God will arise to his rest and we his people—his family—will be clothed with righteousness and shout aloud for joy![139]

The Lord will abundantly bless our provision and satisfy our every desire as he clothes us with salvation.[140] This is what will attract the "fish" to our "nets" and into our "boats." It is the fruit of the incarnation of truth.

It is written, "The fruit of the righteous is a tree of life, and he who wins souls is wise."[141] Access to the tree of life is restored for those who live in the revelation of the incarnation of truth.

The family model is what will win the world to Christ. Is it not written that "wisdom is justified by all her children"?[142] How can all men be brothers apart from the Fatherhood of God? Let's show the world who our Father is by manifesting the incarnation of truth in our own lives. Then they will see Jesus, the author and finisher of our faith and come home to Father's house. This is the model that works! The spirit of God has been sent forth into our hearts and we cry out, "Abba Father!"[143]

> Therefore whoever hears these sayings of Mine, and does them, I will liken him to a wise man who built his house on the rock.
>
> Matthew 7:24

THE FAMILY
MAIN POINTS:

- Jesus declared, "I will build my church."
- The summation of all things accomplished by the incarnation of truth will always add up to be the "family" of God.
- The people of the family of God are his laborers in the harvest of men's souls.
- The harvest can be compared to "fishing for men."
- Too many of the church's nets are breaking and too many of its boats are sinking.
- The church can be described as:
    - a body,
    - a bride,
    - a temple,
    - an army,
    - and a family.
- It is not scriptural to use a business model for the church.
- The "rock" that Jesus will build his church upon is the revelation that he is the Christ, the Son of the living God.
- This revelation is based on a family model for the church.

- Of all the names and titles given to Jesus, when the Father speaks to him or of him from heaven, he calls him "my Son."
- The summation of the words of Jesus all point to the Father and his relationship with him that is now available to us through the completed work of the incarnation of truth.
- The threefold purpose for the incarnation of truth is to:
  - take away our sins,
  - destroy the works of the devil,
  - and restore man to a glorious unity with God.
- Paul described his apostolic, prophetic team ministry using the analogy of a mother and father, which clearly speaks of "family."
- The family model for the church is God's original model.
- It is the lives of God's family members that will ripen the harvest by turning the disobedient to the wisdom of the just.
- Wisdom is justified by all her children.
- The church must be built upon the rock.

EPILOGUE

For the message of the cross is foolishness to those who are perishing, but to us who are being saved it is the power of God.

1 Corinthians 1:18

For as the days of a tree, so shall be the days of My people . . .

Isaiah 65:22b

We have journeyed together a long way. I trust that you have prospered as I certainly have. There remains one final step to take together before we move on to the mountaintop—the place where everyone must get to alone. When I say "alone," I don't mean on your own or without the ushering presence of God.

A true father, especially our heavenly Father, has no greater joy than to hear that his children walk in truth.[1] It is the message of the cross that leads us into the power of truth that makes us really free.[2]

Our precious Lord Jesus went the way of the cross into the hands of men who killed him by hanging him on a tree.[3] Trees are important in the lives of God's people. In the Garden of Eden, there was a choice to be made concerning trees.[4] The days of God's people can be likened to the days of a tree and all the events that surround it.[5]

The cross of our Lord was made from a tree and it has become the focal point of all human history. In the Garden of Gethsemane, our Lord Jesus made a choice that forever reversed the curse that came from the wrong choice made by the first man Adam in the Garden of Eden.

Adam chose the tree that brought death.[6] It was the wrong choice. Jesus chose the tree that brought life *through* death and destroyed him who had the power of death.[7] It was the right choice.

In the Garden of Gethsemane, Jesus accepted his Father's will and placed himself completely into the Father's hands.[8] This was no small thing as the Father had a plan that would require something even greater than placing oneself in his own loving hands. Take note—it will be the same plan that the Father has designed for you and me.

Immediately after surrendering himself to the will of the Father, the Father delivered Jesus into the hands of man![9] This is the way of the tree—of the cross. It wasn't enough for Jesus to be killed. He had to willingly lay down his life into the hands of men and be executed by their hands.[10]

This is the way of glory. It is the way each of us must travel to be able to bring glory to God. It is the way of the cross—the Master's plan. The apostle Paul described it this way: "But God forbid that I should boast except in the cross of our Lord Jesus Christ, by whom the world has been crucified to me, and I to the world."[11] Are you willing to travel this path into the will of God, into the hands of men? What does it mean to have the world crucified to you and you to the world?

What I am describing is the plan of God for the three (excellent) great trees in my life and in yours—me, myself, and I. I will call them "Beauty, Strength, and Stature." These three are common to the lives of all people. Let's examine them.

Who among the multitudes of people filling the earth is really free from the vanity of self-awareness? It is a human condition to be obsessed with our own image. We all want to be beautiful. We all admire beauty. To be beautiful is glorious.

It is easy to understand why. The opposite of beautiful is ugly! This is what fuels the world's multi-billion dollar fashion and cosmetic industry.

We all are concerned with how we look. The truth is that the way of the cross, though very, very "ugly," is the only way to real beauty. To be ugly is a shame (the opposite of glory), but Jesus chose to go that way for our benefit. It is written, "...for the joy that was set before Him endured the cross, despising the shame, and has sat down at the right hand of the throne of God."[12]

The joy set before him was about our real beauty. God beautifies the meek with salvation that comes through the way of the tree.[13] The way of the cross brings the glory of beauty to fruition. The truth is, it is the "Christ in you, [that is] the hope of glory."[14]

The sibling of Beauty is Strength. Who among the multitudes of people filling the earth is really free from the threat of being weak and helpless? It is a human condition to want to be strong. We all admire and exalt ability. "Yes I can" will always be more desirable than "I just cannot."

This is what fuels the world's obsession for power and control. It is the source of slavery, bondage, oppression, and depression. This is what creates the division between the "haves" and the "have-nots."

Everyone wants to be strong. The truth is the way of the cross looks very much like the weakest, most helpless condition a human being could experience. Nevertheless, Jesus chose to go that way for us. He knew that it was the only way to carry the ark of God's heavy presence back into the lives of everyone who would yield their own strength to God's. It is only through the way of the cross that "I can do all things through Christ who strengthens me."[15]

The third sibling in the trinity of me, myself, and I is Stature. Who among the multitudes of people filling the earth is really free from the fear of being alone, unknown, or unrecognized? It is a human condition to want to belong. It is a deep-rooted need.

This is what fuels the world's quest for fame and fortune. To be swallowed up in insignificance and obscurity makes the world a dark, unloving place. It can produce hopelessness—a fatal disease of the heart.[16] It can be worse than death. It's as if one were dead while still being alive.

The quest for stature leads to idolatry as people begin to worship themselves and others whom they exalt above measure. It is the source of pride. What others think and say about such a one becomes more important than what the loving Creator, Redeemer has said.

The only way out of this dilemma is the way that Jesus chose—the way of the tree—the cross. He made himself of no reputation (stature) and took the form of a servant.[17] And so it is written concerning his stature:

> Therefore God also has highly exalted Him and given Him the name which is above every name, that at the name of Jesus every knee should bow, of those in heaven, and of those on earth, and of those under the earth, and that every tongue should confess that Jesus Christ is Lord, to the glory of God the Father.[18]

And so likewise our own three trees of Beauty, Strength, and Stature must yield to the plan of God in order for us to really experience the fullness of all that he has planned for us. God's ways are higher than our ways.[19] Much higher.

God's ultimate intention for us, described in a metaphor, is that we be "trees of righteousness, the planting of the LORD, that He may be glorified."[20] The life of a tree is very interesting, though I imagine few really ever meditate on it. It can be quite like the life of a person.

A tree's life starts as a seed of course, and then springs up as a sapling. Through many long years of this and that it grows to its full size. During those years, it experiences the light of the sun, the light of the moon, and even the light of the stars. Days and nights pass again and again. The tree experiences "time." God "has made everything beautiful in its time."[21]

Heat, cold, rain, and snow are just a few of the extremes the tree has to endure. Birds may nest in it. Snakes may slither up its branches. Dogs may stop by and "you know what" at its base. Has something like that ever happened to you?

Little children may climb all over it and swing from ropes on it. I guess that's not so bad, but can you imagine what it feels like when someone takes a penknife and decides to carve their initials into its bark? Uh-oh, I think I'm talking about my life now, or maybe yours? What about those folks with the bows and arrows? Don't they know that it hurts? It can hurt really badly, can't it? Let's not say much about the axes and chainsaws!

Because of all that, it goes through, especially in winter, the me, myself, and I of a tree, can go from Beauty, Strength, and Stature to ugly, weak, and forgotten very quickly. That happens most around Christmas time, doesn't it? Culturally, that's the time that we celebrate the incarnation of truth, isn't it? Hmmm, this is food for thought.

As I get ready to leave you and continue on towards the mountaintop, this would be a great time to remember that Jesus was a carpenter, a worker of wood.[22] In fact, he is a master carpenter! You can "certainly" trust him with the three trees of your life as I do with mine. I hope you have benefited from what you have read.

I'll close now by recounting an "excellent" traditional folktale by an unknown author. I'll leave it up to you to decide for yourself the source of its "incarnation." It's called "The Tale of Three Trees."

Once upon a mountaintop, three little trees stood and dreamed of what they wanted to be when they grew up.

The first little tree looked up at the stars twinkling like diamonds above him. "I want to hold treasure," he said. "I want to be covered with gold and filled with precious stones. I will be the most beautiful treasure chest in the world!"

The second little tree looked out at the small stream trickling by on its way to the ocean. "I want to be a strong sailing ship," he said. "I want to travel mighty waters and carry powerful kings. I will be the strongest ship in the world!"

The third little tree looked down into the valley below where busy men and busy women worked in a busy town. "I don't want to leave this mountaintop at all," she said. "I want to grow so tall that when people stop to look at me they will raise their eyes to heaven and think of God. I will be the tallest tree in the world!"

Years passed. The rains came, the sun shone, and the little trees grew tall. One day three woodcutters climbed the mountain.

The first woodcutter looked at the first tree and said, "This tree is beautiful. It is perfect for me." With a swoop of his shining axe, the first tree fell.

"Now I shall be made into a beautiful chest," thought the first tree. "I shall hold wonderful treasure."

The second woodcutter looked at the second tree and said, "This tree is strong. It is perfect for me." With a swoop of his shining axe, the second tree fell.

"Now I shall sail mighty waters," thought the second tree. "I shall be a strong ship fit for kings!"

The third tree felt her heart sink when the last woodcutter looked her way. She stood straight and tall and pointed bravely to heaven.

But the woodcutter never even looked up. "Any kind of tree will do for me," he muttered. With a swoop of his shining axe, the third tree fell.

The first tree rejoiced when the woodcutter brought him to a carpenter's shop, but the busy carpenter was not thinking about treasure chests. Instead his work-worn hands fashioned the tree into a feed box for animals.

The once-beautiful tree was not covered with gold or filled with treasure. He was coated with sawdust and filled with hay for hungry farm animals.

The second tree smiled when the woodcutter took him to a shipyard, but no mighty sailing ships were being made that day. Instead the once-strong tree was hammered and sawed into a simple fishing boat.

Too small and too weak to sail an ocean or even a river, he was taken to a little lake. Every day he brought in loads of dead, smelly fish.

The third tree was confused when the woodcutter cut her into strong beams and left her in a lumber yard.

"What happened?" the once-tall tree wondered. "All I ever wanted to do was stay on the mountaintop and point to God."

Many, many days and nights passed. The three trees nearly forgot their dreams.

But one night golden starlight poured over the first tree as a young woman placed her newborn baby in the feed box.

"I wish I could make a cradle for him," her husband whispered. The mother squeezed his hand and smiled as the starlight shone on the smooth and sturdy wood. "This manger is beautiful," she said.

And suddenly the first tree knew he was holding the greatest treasure in the world.

One evening a tired traveler and his friends crowded into the old fishing boat. The traveler fell asleep as the second tree quietly sailed out into the lake.

Soon a thundering and thrashing storm arose. The little tree shuddered. He knew he did not have the strength to carry so many passengers safely through the wind and rain.

The tired man awakened. He stood up, stretched out his hand, and said, "Peace." The storm stopped as quickly as it had begun.

And suddenly the second tree knew he was carrying the King of heaven and earth.

[Then one] morning, the third tree was startled when her beams were yanked out from the forgotten woodpile. She flinched as she was carried through an angry, jeering crowd. She shuddered when soldiers nailed a man's hands to her.

She felt ugly and harsh and cruel.

But [three days later], when the sun rose and the earth trembled with joy beneath her, the third tree knew that God's love had changed everything.

It had made the first tree beautiful.

It had made the second tree strong.

And every time people thought of the third tree, they would think of God.

[Unto] Him be glory in the church by Christ Jesus to all generations, forever and ever. Amen.

Ephesians 3:21

<u>EPILOGUE</u>

MAIN POINTS:

- The life of God's people can be likened to the days of a tree.
- The way of the cross is the way of the tree.
- Adam chose a tree that brought death.
- Jesus chose a tree that brought life through death.
- Jesus first surrendered to His Father and then to the hands of man.
- Beauty, Strength, and Stature are three desires and needs of man.
- The way of the cross is the only way to fulfill these desires and needs.
- Jesus is the Master Carpenter

ENDNOTES

PROLOGUE

1 John 8.32.
2 QuickVerse 2007. Vers. 11.0.0.
  Hebrew Dictionary. Word #7991.
3 Isaiah 48:16; 2 Corinthians 13:14
4 John 14:6; 1 John 1:5; 1 John 4:8
5 Genesis 1:27
6 1 Thessalonians 5:23
7 Deuteronomy 16:16
8 Exodus 40:2-8; Hebrews 9:1-5; Revelation 11:1-2
9 Exodus 40:33; Hebrews 9:2, 5
10 Matthew 6:11
11 Luke 24:19; Hebrews 7:20-22; John 18:37
12 John 14:6
13 Revelation 19:13
14 Scofield, Rev. C.I., et al. *The Scofield Reference Bible*, KJV. New York: Oxford UP, 1945. Luke 4:4; 1 Peter 2:2; Hebrews 5:12-14
15 Mark 4:28
16 Mark 4:20
17 Genesis 1:28
18 Genesis 13:16; 22:17; 15:5
19 Romans 12:2
20 Malachi 3:8-10; Matthew 6:3-4
21 1 John 5:7-8
22 Proverbs 22:21

23   Ecclesiastes 4:9a
24   Ecclesiastes 4:12b paraphrased
25   Job 32:5
26   Job 33:18
27   Job 33:1-4
28   Job 33:14-16
29   Job 33:29-30
30   Matthew 7:7

THE QUESTIONS
1   John 14:16
2   Revelation 1:8; Hebrews 12:2
3   John 5:39
4   Romans 15:4
5   Ephesians 1:3a
6   John 1:18; 10:30
7   2 Corinthians 13:14
8   Ephesians 1:3b
9   Genesis 2:1; Hebrews 1:7; Psalm 103:20
10   Ephesians 1:4a
11   Isaiah 46:9-10
12   Ephesians 3:11
13   Revelation 1:8
14   Genesis 1:1
15   Matthew 6:9-10
16   Revelation 4:1-2; Psalm 45:6
17   Psalm 11:4; 103:19; Isaiah 66:1
18   Ephesians 1:3b
19   Colossians 1:16
20   Isaiah 66:1
21   Genesis 1:1

22 Genesis 3:1-24
23 Hebrews 9:15; Revelation 5:9
24 Acts 3:21
25 Ephesians 1:5, 7 paraphrased
26 John 14:6
27 Ibid
28 Ephesians 1:4b
29 Psalm 99:5
30 1 Peter 1:15-16
31 Genesis 1:27
32 Proverbs 25:2 paraphrased
33 Dr. Myles Munroe, Bible teacher and author.
34 Psalm 25:14
35 Deuteronomy 29:29 excerpt
36 Ephesians 1:17
37 Ephesians 1:18-19a
38 Ephesians 3:1-4, 9
39 Ephesians 3:10
40 Ephesians 3:11
41 John 19:30
42 Revelation 21:6
43 2 Timothy 2:19a
44 Isaiah 43:10
45 Ephesians 1:13-14
46 2 Corinthians 5:1, 5
47 Acts 1:8
48 Romans 13:11
49 Ephesians 3:9-10
50 Ephesians 1:4b
51 Ephesians 1:5, 7
52 John 6:63

53   John 8:32
54   Romans 15:4

THE LITTLE CHILDREN

1   John 1:14
2   1 John 3:5
3   1 Peter 1:18
4   1 Peter 1:19
5   Isaiah 53:5-6
6   Hebrews 2:3
7   Romans 3:23
8   Romans 5: 12, 18a, 19a
9   Romans 8:1-2
10   Romans 3:23
11   1 Peter 1:20; Matthew 20:28
12   1 Timothy 2:5-6; John 3:16
13   John 1:29
14   1 John 3:5
15   Ephesians 1:4
16   1 John 4:9-10
17   1 Peter 1:2
18   1 John 3:5
19   John 3:16
20   Titus 1:2
21   Titus 1:3
22   Genesis 1:1-31
23   Romans 1:16
24   1 Corinthians 1:21
25   Brown, Colin., et al. *The New International Dictionary of New Testament Theology*. Exeter,

Devon, U.K.: Paternoster Press, 1986. Vol. 2; 107-108. 4 vols.

26   2 Timothy 1:8

27   2 Timothy 1:9

28   2 Timothy 1:10

29   Ibid

30   Hebrew 9:26b

31   Romans 16:25-26

32   John 1:14

33   John 8:31-32

34   Acts 20:20, 27 excerpts

35   Source unknown

36   Ibid

37   John 1:12

38   Ephesians 6:11

39   2 Corinthians 2:11

40   Name withheld for privacy

41   John 1:12; John 3:7

42   2 Corinthians 5:17

43   1 Corinthians 13:11; John 15:8

44   John 15:8

45   Romans 3:23

46   Mark 4:13

47   Matthew 13:7, 22

48   Genesis 3:17-19

49   Numbers 33:55

50   Numbers 33:56

51   1 John 2:12, 13b

52   Revelation 2:7 excerpt

53   Revelation 2:11 excerpt

54   Revelation 2:17 excerpt

55   Revelation 2:25-28 excerpts
56   Revelation 3:5
57   Revelation 3:12
58   Revelation 3:21
59   Hebrews 6:5
60   Hebrews 5:12-13
61   Luke 8:14 excerpt
62   Matthew 13:22
63   Ibid
64   Mark 4:19
65   Luke 8:14
66   Hebrews 2:10
67   1 John 2:12
68   John 17:17

THE YOUNG MEN

1   1 John 3:5
2   Proverbs 22:20-21
3   1 John 2:12
4   Isaiah 14:12-14; Ezekiel 28:12-19; Jude 6;
      Revelation 12:7
5   Genesis 3:1
6   Psalm 8:4-6
7   Hebrews 2:5
8   John 14:30
9   2 Corinthians 4:4
10   Ephesians 2:2
11   Ephesians 6:12
12   Psalm 8:5
13   Psalm 8:6
14   Genesis 1:26

15   Psalm 115:16
16   Matthew 28:18-19a
17   1 Peter 2:9
18   Psalm 8:2; Matthew 21:16
19   Romans 5:12
20   Genesis 1:28
21   1 Corinthians 15:45-47
22   John 19:30
23   John 8:49
24   Matthew 20:28
25   Romans 8:11
26   Hebrews 2:12
27   Ephesians 3:10-11
28   Colossians 2:15
29   Hebrews 2:14
30   Hebrews 1:6
31   Philippians 2:9-11
32   Revelation 1:18
33   Hebrews 9:14
34   Hebrews 10:2
35   QuickVerse 2007. Vers. 11.0.0. Greek Dictionary. Word #5046.
36   Hebrews 10:1-2, 10-14
37   Romans 12:1
38   Romans 12:2
39   1 Corinthians 2:16
40   Genesis 3:11
41   2 Corinthians 5:17-18a
42   1 John 3:8
43   Colossians 2:15
44   Hebrews 2:14

45 2 Corinthians 2:14

46 QuickVerse 2007. Vers. 11.0.0. Greek Dictionary. Word #554.

47 "invest." Neufeldt, Victoria., et al. *Webster's New World College Dictionary*. New York: Simon & Schuster, 1997.

48 QuickVerse 2007. Vers. 11.0.0. Greek Dictionary. Word #2673.

49 Ibid. Greek Dictionary. Words #691, 692.

50 Psalm 8:2

51 QuickVerse 2007. Vers. 11.0.0. Greek Dictionary. Word #2358.

52 Colossians 2:15; Spirit Filled Life Bible footnote

53 QuickVerse 2007. Vers. 11.0.0. Greek Dictionary. Word #2358.

54 "iamb." Neufeldt, Victoria., et al. *Webster's New World College Dictionary*. New York: Simon & Schuster, 1997.

55 QuickVerse 2007. Vers. 11.0.0. Hebrew Dictionary. Word #8426.

56 Romans 8:37

57 1 John 2:13b

58 Matthew 28:18-20

59 Acts 1:8

60 John 8:31-32

61 Acts 1:1

62 Mark 16:20

63 John 17:15, 17

64 Ibid

65 Luke 9:1; 10:1

66 John 17:20

67   1 John 2:14b
68   Colossians 1:27
69   2 Corinthians 2:14
70   2 Corinthians 3:2-3
71   Romans 8:11
72   Joshua 1:7; Psalm 1:1-3
73   2 Corinthians 3:9; 4:1
74   2 Corinthians 5:18
75   2 Corinthians 4:2; 5:20
76   1 Peter 1:6-7
77   James 1:2-4
78   Hebrews 6:12
79   2 Corinthians 4:1
80   2 Corinthians 4:7
81   John 19:30
82   Galatians 4:19
83   Romans 8:19
84   Romans 8:21
85   Romans 8:18
86   Romans 8:28
87   2 Corinthians 4:7
88   Ibid
89   2 Corinthians 4:8
90   2 Corinthians 4:9
91   2 Corinthians 3:18b
92   2 Corinthians 4:10a
93   Philippians 3:10
94   2 Corinthians 4:10
95   2 Corinthians 4:11
96   Hebrews 2:14b
97   Song of Solomon 8:6a

98   1 John 2:14b
99   John 15:13
100   Colossians 3:3
101   Galatians 2:20
102   Romans 6:7
103   Romans 6:8-9
104   Romans 6:10
105   1 John 4:17
106   Romans 6:11
107   Romans 6:5; 2 Corinthians 4:11
108   2 Corinthians 4:12
109   Hebrews 2:14
110   2 Corinthians 4:16
111   2 Corinthians 4:17a
112   1 Peter 1:6-7
113   2 Corinthians 4:17b
114   2 Corinthians 4:18
115   1 Corinthians 13:7 paraphrased

THE FATHERS
1   1 Peter 1:25
2   Ezekiel 22:14
3   Deuteronomy 5:24
4   Deuteronomy 6:4-9, Spirit Filled Life Bible footnote
5   Deuteronomy 6:4
6   Deuteronomy 6:5; Matthew 22:37-38
7   Deuteronomy 6:6-7
8   1 Peter 2:2
9   Luke 4:4; 1 John 2:14b

10   Scofield, Rev. C.I., et al. *The Scofield Reference Bible*, KJV. New York: Oxford UP, 1945. Hebrews 5:14.

11   John 17:5, 24b

12   Genesis 1:1; 2:1

13   John 1:1-2

14   John 1:14

15   John 1:29

16   1 Peter 1:18-20 excerpts

17   Ephesians 1:4

18   Isaiah 48:16

19   John 10:30-31

20   2 Peter 1:1-4

21   John 17:22

22   Hebrews 2:13b

23   Ephesians 1:4

24   1 John 2:12; 3:5; Ephesians 1:4

25   1 John 2:14; 3:8b; Song of Solomon 8:6

26   John 17:22; 1 John 2:13a; 1 Peter 1:16

27   John 17:17

28   John 17:18

29   John 17:21

30   Ephesians 1:10

31   Ephesians 1:4, 9

32   Hebrews 12:14

33   John 1:14

34   John 1:18

35   Hebrews 2:12

36   Hebrews 2:11

37   Hebrews 2:10

38   John 17:5

39	John 18:37
40	Luke 2:49
41	John 17:4
42	Hebrews 10:7
43	Hebrews 10:10
44	John 6:38
45	John 12:27a
46	Matthew 26:38; Luke 22:44
47	John 12:27-28a
48	John 17:1; 4:5
49	Ecclesiastes 4:12b paraphrased
50	Proverbs 22:20-21
51	John 17:21
52	1 John 2:14a
53	John 15:16
54	John 14:12
55	John 17:18
56	Ephesians 1:4
57	John 15:16
58	John 15:8
59	1 John 1:1-4
60	2 Corinthians 13:14
61	Isaiah 48:16
62	1 John 5:9a
63	1 John 5:7
64	Comprised from John 17 and Hebrews 10:5-7
65	John 17:3
66	Psalm 133:1, 3b
67	1 Corinthians 1:9
68	Hebrews 6:19-20
69	Hebrews 9:24

70   John 20:21-23
71   2 Corinthians 5:17-20
72   Psalm 16:11
73   Luke 2:14
74   Luke 2:10; John 3:16
75   Scofield, Rev. C.I., et al. *The Scofield Reference Bible,* KJV. New York: Oxford UP, 1945. 1 Peter 1:7-8.
76   Source Unknown
77   1 Peter 1:9
78   Ibid
79   John 3:16a
80   Ephesians 4:4-6
81   Ephesians 4:3
82   Ephesians 4:14-15
83   1 Corinthians 4:14-16
84   QuickVerse 2007. Vers. 11.0.0. Greek Dictionary. Word #3402.
85   Ephesians 4:11-12; 1 Corinthians 12:28
86   Isaiah 38:19
87   Psalm 78:1-6 paraphrased
88   Romans 10:10; John 1:12
89   1 Peter 2:2
90   Luke 4:4
91   1 John 2:13-14 paraphrased excerpt
92   Hebrews 5:12-14
93   Romans 13:11
94   Ephesians 4:15
95   2 Peter 1:3
96   2 Peter 1:4

THE JOURNEY

1   Ephesians 4:13 paraphrase
2   Matthew 5:48
3   QuickVerse 2007. Vers. 11.0.0. Greek Dictionary. Word #5046.
4   John 19:30
5   Colossians 1:13
6   1 Peter 2:9
7   Hebrews 6:1-3 excerpts
8   Psalm 119:105
9   Luke 9:1-2
10   Luke 9:3
11   2 Peter 1:12
12   Reverend Tommy Tenney, Bible teacher and author; story recounted as heard
13   Prophetic statement based upon Revelation 22:16; Malachi 3:1; 4:2
14   3 John 4
15   3 John 6 excerpt
16   3 John 7 excerpt
17   Revelation 1:8; Hebrews 12:2
18   Scofield, Rev. C.I., et al. *The Scofield Reference Bible*, KJV. New York: Oxford UP, 1945. Matthew 7:14.
19   QuickVerse 2007. Vers. 11.0.0. Greek Dictionary. Word #5043.
20   Ibid. Word # 3516.
21   Ibid. Word # 3813.
22   Ibid. Word # 3495.
23   Ibid. Word #5207.
24   Ibid. Word # 3962.

25   Ibid. Word # 5046.

26   Proverbs 25:2

27   2 Timothy 2:15 KJV and NKJV paraphrase

28   Deuteronomy 29:29

29   John 3:3, 7; 2 Corinthians 5:17

30   Acts 1:8; 2:40; 8:25; 10:42, etc.

31   Proverbs 13:24

32   Proverbs 23:13-14

33   QuickVerse 2007. Vers. 11.0.0. Greek Dictionary. Word #3813.

34   Proverbs 22:15

35   Proverbs 20:30

36   Proverbs 27:6

37   Acts 2:17 excerpt

38   QuickVerse 2007. Vers. 11.0.0. Greek Dictionary. Words #3706 and #3708.

39   Acts 6:11

40   Acts 7:57-58

41   Acts 8:1

42   QuickVerse 2007. Vers. 11.0.0. Greek Dictionary. Word #3494.

43   Ibid. Word #2012.

44   Ibid. Word #3623.

45   Ibid. Words #5206 and #5207.

46   Ibid. Word #1080.

47   John 15:13

48   Deuteronomy 30:5

49   1 Corinthians 15:10

50   1 Corinthians 15:58

51   Philippians 3:12

52   Philippians 3:14-15

53 Matthew 4:19a
54 Philippians 3:17
55 Ephesians 4:13
56 Ibid
57 Ephesians 4:3
58 Ephesians 1:14
59 Ephesians 1:13
60 John 14:16
61 John 14:16-17
62 Ibid
63 John 14:26
64 Ibid
65 John 15:26
66 John 16:8
67 John 16:13
68 Ibid
69 Ibid
70 John 16:14
71 Ibid
72 Neufeldt, Victoria., et al. *Webster's New World College Dictionary*. New York: Simon & Schuster, 1997. "teleology."

THE FAMILY

1 QuickVerse 2007. Vers. 11.0.0. Greek Dictionary. Word #3965.
2 Ibid. Word #3962.
3 John 5:26
4 Matthew 6:9
5 Genesis 1:27

6   QuickVerse 2007. Vers. 11.0.0. Greek Dictionary. Word #3966.
7   2 Corinthians 5:17
8   Matthew 16:18 excerpt
9   QuickVerse 2007. Vers. 11.0.0. Greek Dictionary. Word #1577.
10   1 Peter 2:9
11   Ibid
12   Scofield, Rev. C.I., et al. *The Scofield Reference Bible*, KJV. New York: Oxford UP, 1945. James 5:7.
13   Matthew 9:36-38
14   Matthew 4:19
15   Matthew 13:47-50
16   Habakkuk 2:14
17   John 3:16
18   Luke 5:9
19   Luke 5:1-3
20   Luke 5:10
21   Luke 5:4
22   Luke 5:5
23   Luke 5:6
24   Luke 5:7
25   Matthew 16:18
26   Dr. Myles Munroe; heard at Rock Church of Virginia Beach, 1990
27   Romans 10:17
28   Job 34:3
29   1 Corinthians 12:27
30   1 Corinthians 12:18
31   Ephesians 5:32

32   Ephesians 5:22-29

33   Revelations 21:9

34   Revelations 19:6-7

35   1 Peter 2:5

36   Ephesians 2:19-22

37   Ephesians 6:11-12

38   Ephesians 3:9-11

39   Ephesians 3:14-15

40   Ephesians 5:23

41   1 Peter 2:6-7

42   Hebrews 2:10

43   Joshua 5:14; perhaps a Christophany; a pre-incarnate manifestation of Christ

44   Ephesians 4:12

45   Ephesians 4:11

46   Ephesians 4:13

47   2 Corinthians 11:12

48   Deuteronomy 8:18

49   Leviticus 3:3

50   Leviticus 23:24-25

51   Exodus 31:14

52   Matthew 16:18 excerpt

53   Matthew 16:13

54   Matthew 16:15

55   Matthew 16:16

56   Matthew 16:17

57   QuickVerse 2007. Vers. 11.0.0. Greek Dictionary. Word # 4073.

58   QuickVerse 2007. Vers. 11.0.0. Greek Dictionary. Word # 4074.

59   Luke 24:19

60   Hebrews 7:17
61   Revelation 17:14
62   Revelation 17:14; 19:16
63   Revelation 1:8; 21:6
64   Ibid
65   Hebrews 12:2
66   John 1:29
67   Revelation 22:16
68   Matthew 16:27; 17:12; Revelation 14:14
69   Revelation 19:13
70   Revelation 19:11
71   Isaiah 9:6
72   Ibid
73   Ibid
74   Ibid
75   Ibid
76   Revelation 5:5
77   Ibid
78   Zechariah 3:8
79   Matthew 3:13
80   Matthew 3:3
81   Luke 1:17 excerpt
82   Ibid
83   Malachi 4:6 excerpt
84   QuickVerse 2007. Vers. 11.0.0. Greek Dictionary.
      Words #600 and #2325.
85   Matthew 17:11
86   John 1:29 excerpt
87   Matthew 3:14
88   Matthew 3:15

89   Matthew 3:16
90   Matthew 3:17
91   Matthew 17:1-2
92   Luke 9:30-31
93   Matthew 17:15
94   John 10:30; 14:6b; 14:2; 14:21b; 14:23
95   John 17:1; Matthew 6:7-13
96   Romans 8:19
97   John 16:25
98   John 14:6
99   Genesis 2:18
100   Genesis 2:21-22
101   John 19:33-34; Ephesians 5:30
102   2 Corinthians 5:20
103   Acts 13:1-3
104   Psalm 34:8
105   1 Thessalonians 2:4
106   1 Thessalonians 2:6
107   1 Thessalonians 2:7-8
108   Acts 16:16-18
109   Acts 19:11-12
110   Romans 2:16
111   1 Thessalonians 2:11
112   QuickVerse 2007. Vers. 11.0.0. Greek Dictionary.
      Word #3870.
113   QuickVerse 2007. Vers. 11.0.0. Greek Dictionary.
      Word #3888.
114   QuickVerse 2007. Vers. 11.0.0. Greek Dictionary.
      Word #3844.
115   Isaiah 38:19

116   QuickVerse 2007. Vers. 11.0.0. Greek Dictionary. Word #3144.
117   Based on 1 Thessalonians 2:11
118   Galatians 2:20
119   1 Thessalonians 2:13
120   Matthew 18:19-20
121   1 Timothy 3:1-5
122   Ephesians 3:9-10
123   Luke 1:17; Malachi 4:5-6
124   Psalm 68:5-6a
125   Malachi 4:5-6
126   Luke 1:16-17
127   John 1:29
128   Luke 3:4-6
129   Matthew 13:22; Mark 4:19; Luke 8:14
130   Ephesians 6:2-3 excerpt
131   Deuteronomy 6:7
132   Deuteronomy 1:11
133   Revelation 19:10b
134   Deuteronomy 30:5
135   Genesis 1:28
136   Luke 1:17
137   2 Corinthians 5:21
138   A compilation from Proverbs 1:20-23; 3:13-18, 35a; 8:1-7a, 35; 9:1; 16:16a; 24:3a, 13-14; 29:3a
139   Psalm 132:8-9
140   Psalm 132:15-16
141   Proverbs 11:30
142   Luke 7:35
143   Galatians 4:6

EPILOGUE

1   3 John 4
2   1 Corinthians 1:18; John 8:32
3   Acts 10:39
4   Genesis 2:16-17
5   Isaiah 65:22b
6   Genesis 3:6, 12
7   Hebrews 2:14
8   Luke 22:42
9   Matthew 26:43-50
10 John 10:18
11 Galatians 6:14
12 Hebrews 12:2
13 Psalm 149:4
14 Colossians 1:27
15 Philippians 4:13
16 Proverbs 13:12
17 Philippians 2:7
18 Philippians 2:9-11
19 Isaiah 55:8-9
20 Isaiah 61:3
21 Ecclesiastes 3:11
22 Mark 6:3